Laughter, Love & Limits

PARENTING FOR LIFE

DR. MAGGIE MAMEN

 Published by Creative Bound Inc.
P.O. Box 424, Carp, Ontario
Canada K0A 1L0
(613) 831-3641

ISBN 0-921165-54-4
Printed and bound in Canada
Copyright © 1998, 2003 Maggie Mamen

This book is not intended to replace appropriate diagnosis and/or treatment, when indicated, by a qualified mental health professional or physician. Any names used as examples throughout this book have been changed to ensure the privacy of individuals and families.

Book design by Wendelina O'Keefe.
Cover photographs © PhotoDisc 1998

Canadian Cataloguing in Publication Data

Mamen, Maggie
      Laughter, love and limits : parenting for life

Includes bibliographical references.
ISBN 0-921165-54-4

      1. Parenting. I. Title.

HQ755.8.M34 1998   649'.1   C98-901164-X

For Mum (1910-1976) and Dad (1916-1979)
for being the best they could be
and
for Max (1985-1998)
for the unconditional love he brought to our family

My child. My daughter. I don't have all the answers for you, Margaret. Most of the time I feel that I'm merely an older version of a child myself. I'm afraid, but I cannot show you my fear. I despair, but I cannot share my sorrow. You see me as strong—the master of my life and my fate—while all the time I feel as though at any moment the unmasking will occur and the world will see me—and you will see me—as I really am, weak and riven by doubt. You want me to be understanding. You want me to tell you how things are going to be. You want me to make things right—life right—by waving the wand of my indignation over injustice and over your hurts, and I can't do that. I don't even know how.

Mothering isn't something one learns, Maggie. It's something one does. It doesn't come naturally to any woman because there is nothing natural about having a life completely dependent upon one's own. It's the only kind of employment that exists in which one can feel so utterly necessary and at the same moment so entirely alone. And in moments of crisis—like this one, Maggie—there is no sagacious volume in which one looks up answers and thus discovers how to prevent a child from harming herself.

Children do more than steal one's heart, my dear. They steal one's life. They elicit the worst and the best that we have to offer, and in return they offer their trust. But the cost of all this is insurmountably high and the rewards are small and long in coming.

And at the end, when one prepares to release the infant, the child, the adolescent into adulthood, it is with the hope that what remains behind is something bigger—and more—than Mummy's empty arms.

From: *Missing Joseph* by Elizabeth George

Table of Contents

Prologue

Raising children seems to come easily to some women—and to some men. The rest of us muddle along as best we can—a touch of instinct here, a tad of common sense there, a few dollops of solicited or unsolicited advice—and parenting books to fill the gaps in the seats of our pants. We may recognize ourselves in the quotation at the beginning of the book—in the almost universal dilemma of having to be at our most competent in a job for which we have no training and precious little forewarning of what is to come. Plus there is the added dimension of discovering that, once we have learned the answers to at least some of the questions with our first child, the second arrives with a different set of wants and needs, and we start over again, no more wise, although perhaps a little less foolish.

While many of us are in a hurry to find the tools we need to raise our children in this ever-more-complex world, we sometimes run into the perennial problem of "more haste, less speed," trying to implement strategies to make changes before we have really examined what it is we want to change and, more important, why we want to change it. There is some wisdom in first taking a step backwards and examining the overall job we are trying to do, as well as what we expect of our children at their various stages of development.

Consider the difference between the verbs "to mother" and "to father." While both women and men can "mother" in terms of nurturing, protecting and raising children, women are, as yet, unable to "father" children. The latter has its limits in biology; the former does not. The need to be fathered precedes life itself, and yet to be mothered seems more universal in terms of what children need for their overall development and mental health. We must be extremely careful, however, not to fall into the trap of assuming that mothering is exclusively women's work. What about the women who don't want to mother? Are they unnatural? What about the men who do? Are *they*? What if you louse it up—are you a failure? Who says what being a "good mother" is all about? Who says you have to be female to nurture? How come some "good mothers" have difficult kids and some wonderful kids have apparently inadequate mothers? How come children need their fathers so much?

We—male or female—may love our children fiercely and even like them most of the time. We may yearn to do a good job and agonize over each decision. We may be overcome with anxiety at the thought of all that can go wrong. We may experience a child who responds well to our efforts, and yet another who spurns the very same approaches. We may have a child who is hard to like. We may at times want to quit the job, realize what a trap we are in and despair. We may taste the sweet nectar of accomplishment only when they are sound asleep or when they are all grown up—or we may be one of the lucky ones who sees joy day by day. Whatever we are, male or female, we are all mothers to our children. Motherhood is not a gender issue.

This book is about the many aspects of parenting—whether we are male or female and whatever the ages of our children may be. It is not so much a "how-to" book as a "what-is-it-all-about?" book and for some a "gee-whiz-I-thought-I-was-the-only-one-who-felt-that!" book—but you will hopefully find some practical, constructive ideas in its pages. The idea that we can find something funny in the serious business of raising children is appealing. This is especially true for those of us who spend many days wondering if our sense of humor has unwittingly been surgically removed. The themes of love and laughter are interwoven with the stories telling of families not that unlike our own.

The term "Parenting for Life" has two aspects. Firstly, for those of us who are parents, it is a life-long commitment, continuing way after our children have left the nest. Its facets change; its mosaic is always dynamic, never static, and it is at its most intense, of course, during its first two decades. Yet, even when our children have moved into adulthood, we seem to have a never-ending, constantly evolving role to play in their lives. Secondly, parenting is a function that is *essential* to the lives of our children. True mental health is built on the foundations of a solid family that provides a safe haven during those long and sometimes difficult struggles from dependence to independence. We know that, without nurturing, children can wither and fade, physically and mentally, even before they are born.

We also know that love alone is not enough—that children also need guidance and leadership if they are to complete the journey successfully through infancy, childhood and adolescence. Setting limits for children so that they may learn the necessary skills required for life outside the family is a fundamental component of parenting. Research over the past several decades has shown us that the best-adjusted children come from parents who are warm and loving, but who are also willing to place boundaries around their children—to provide some expectations of appropriate behavior, be it related to daily life or to lifetime values—within which the children can explore and grow. Children who have no limits simply drift. Children who have no limits within the family may find the world outside the family extraordinarily difficult and scary, or they may see it as a place where any limits they encounter are to be manipulated or ignored.

We shall explore, and perhaps even dispel, some of the myths that surround the serious business of motherhood—and parenthood in general. In our search for laughter and love, we shall visit maternal instinct—perhaps the greatest of all the myths—to see who has it and what happens for those who do not, taking a peek at how it can work both for and agin us, including some of the dangers inherent in believing in it wholeheartedly—such as omitting half the human race from instinctive parenting and burdening the other half with immeasurable guilt.

Many of the myths of parenting are passed on primarily by our children and our children's children in their eternal hunt for pleasure and the easy way, and in their quest to return their siblings from whence they came. As with most myths, they all contain a kernel of truth; the eternal dilemma and quest of parents rest in using reasonable judgment in appropriate circumstances in their children's best interests. As if we know how to do that! Self-confidence as a parent is something that most of us lack; usually because we get very little feedback on our performance and mostly because we assume the worst. So when our children challenge us, particularly when they hit adolescence, we realize that we have been discovered. Like the Wizard of

Oz, a tiny person behind a large facade, we are trying to do a job for which, much of the time, we feel woefully lacking in competence.

The latter portions of the book are dedicated to what the job of parenting is all about: the goals of parenthood in an era that is at the threshold of the future. Our children are being raised in a world that is becoming increasingly unfamiliar to us—just as our world has been for our parents—filled with so many possibilities that everyone can simply become overwhelmed. This is the inevitable march of time. In this world of mass media, we need more and more to look within our families at what we are doing and why, and how we can maintain the core of values that are essential for human beings "living humanly" in the midst of, and perhaps even despite, the onslaught of contradictory messages and value systems. Children need, and sometimes desperately search for, stepping stones in the quicksand of their lives. As parents, it is our job to provide these anchors and limits until our children can provide them for themselves. They will test us many times along the way to see if they can trust what we are teaching them, but they will be safe and secure knowing that we are guiding them through.

It is hard, if not impossible, to set parenting goals and priorities that are universal because of the truly interactive mosaic of the parent-child interaction. With each child, we create a different mosaic. Each child has different needs, not only from each other child, but even within themselves from day to day. We are sometimes in tune with their needs. Sometimes other parts of our lives take priority. However, children cannot wait until we all have our lives in order. They have the right to be parented and they have the need to be parented *now*. The basic right of children to be nurtured and protected—to be "mothered," whoever takes on that role—is a given.

The book ends with the three big goals of parenting—those that can guide us as we muddle through. The final of these is accompanied by a heartfelt plea based on more than a decade of meeting, almost daily, with adolescents, and even occasionally with children as young as six or seven, who feel that this world is a place they would prefer not to be. I am deliberately picking it out and paraphrasing it here; just in case you are just browsing and don't buy the book, or in case you do buy it but don't get as far as the final goal! This plea is to provide our children with some hope for the future: to show them the half of the glass that is full; to find, develop and share our passion and joy for life; and to let them see that becoming an adult is something worth striving for. In this way, we can be sure that our job as a parent has been done, when our fledglings leave the nest to make their own way in the world they will be part of creating.

We shall visit a number of mothers, fathers and children in the course of this book. In the interests of confidentiality and for the convenience of illustrating particular issues, the names and details of the stories have been changed; the messages have not. If you recognize yourself here, it is not necessarily because we know each other. Your experiences, along with those of all the families I have the privilege to meet every day of my life, continue to provide an eerie sense of universality whilst maintaining the rich tapestry of individual differences

There are as always many thanks to be shared. To Gail Baird, my editor and publisher, for your patience, support and constant enthusiasm in guiding me through the jungles of journalism. To Danny, for the unique and enriching experience of knowing you, thereby of being more able to understand the profound need a child has to be mothered and of discovering the extraordinary lengths to which a child will go to recover that mother so that she can fulfill such a need. To our own three children, Natalie, Katy and Jorin, for enabling me to muddle through and for becoming awesome adults. Finally, to my very own surrogate "mother," the one who protects and nurtures me, keeps me safe, rubs my back, tells me stories, is there for me in the middle of the night when I waken from a bad dream, and says he loves me T-H-I-S much—my husband Rolf.

Chapter 1

Take My Parents...Please!

You Have to Laugh...

I grew up in a home full of laughter. Dad would get what Mom called his "soppy look" on his face and we all knew that a joke was coming; usually a play on words, frequently a bad pun, sometimes one that he could carry on for several minutes, sometimes a long, long shaggy-dog story full of repetition and predictable phrases and punchlines which we all chanted on cue. By the end, Mom would be speechless with laughter, legs crossed, tears rolling down her cheeks, and we would be giggling as much at her response as at whatever had started the joke in the first place. She was his "straight man." She set him up, fed him the right cues, and played right into his hands every time. We all loved it. My sister, a gifted mimic, would have us howling at her impressions of various teachers, relatives and even the odd member of the church congregation. At Christmas time every year, we put on a pantomime in the front room. Aunty Dolly, who was a court dressmaker, would make fairy dresses out of leftover tulle, complete with wings and a wand with a silver star, and one magical year a pair of ballet slippers. Dad's costume somehow always incorporated two saucepan lids and a silly hat. There was no script and it was never quite clear who were the players and who was the audience. Yet we all laughed until we ached, even though we probably couldn't tell you what we found so funny.

Dad loved to listen to comedians on the radio and to watch them on TV. He would start to giggle at the beginning of the signature tune for the *Goon Show* and *Hancock's Half Hour* before a single word had been spoken. He anticipated all the jokes, knew some of the scripts off by heart and laughed as heartily and as sincerely at the twelfth time through as he did at the first. He was also a born performer. He regaled the church congregation at various concerts through the year, often dressed in outrageous clothing, producing glaringly obvious parodies that included thinly disguised local characters, and taking liberties with the planned scripts. I believe that I inherited my love of performance from him. I can remember his teaching me one of his shaggy-dog stories at a very young age. I would recite it at the drop of the proverbial hat to any adults who would listen, to roars of laughter from the audience. It was only when I grew up that I finally realized that the punchline "Never lose your head over a little bit of fluff" had anything to do with anything other than bunnies. By age 11, I was reciting *Albert and the Lion* like a pro, telling the gory, cautionary tale of a poor young boy who was dragged through the bars of a cage and swallowed whole as a consequence of poking the somnolent animal in the ear with an umbrella. His mother, when asked if she would have more children following Albert's sad demise, responded "What? Waste all my life raising children/To feed bloody lions—not me!" The subtle commentary on parenting was totally lost on me. Despite the fact that the final line was censored to substitute the word "blinking" which was considered to be more appropriate for its 11-year-old presenter, the listeners would roar time after predictable time. The wonderful high from being able to elicit laughter from an audience has never quite worn off.

Mom and Dad even laughed about the war, although they were married on Dad's first leave and spent almost six years never knowing if they would see the other again, each and every time they said good-bye. Mom would laugh about the blackouts, about bumping into lamp-posts in the pitch dark; about giggling with her office mates as they hid under their desks while the Buzz Bombs went overhead until the "all-clear" sounded; about Granddad going home to his bed every night from the bomb shelters during the Blitz. He said that if a bomb was going to get him, it would get him wherever he was, so he might as well be comfortable. Dad would laugh about smuggling butter and eggs (both strictly rationed) from the farmlands of Scotland to the deprivation of London and dropping his suitcase in Trafalgar Square while he was running to catch a bus; about not seeing any action, "not a single

Gerry plane," where he was posted in the Orkneys and the Shetlands way north of Scotland, and only finding out what the war was all about by coming home on leave; about learning every card game in the world to pass the time while he was on active service; and about the beginnings of the show-business side of his personality, entertaining the other troops with vaudeville and music hall acts that he remembered word for word and note for note until the day he died. They even laughed about the fact that Dad was a huge-hearted pacifist whose fitness rating kept him out of active service. He always maintained that his flat feet had saved his life.

As a child, I remember listening from my bed at night, hearing Mom and Dad giggling about something my sister or I had said or done. I remember catching them glancing at each other and looking away so as not to make each other crumple into paroxysms of mirth. I remember the righteous indignation I felt as a teenager, yelling at them "What? What? What's so funny?" when I was the perceived victim of an unspoken comment or look. One of Mom's favorite responses was "Well, you have to laugh, or you'd cry."

It wasn't until much later that it became obvious to me that their lives were not all light and funny and that denial sometimes makes a great coping strategy. Dad himself had been sent away to foster care when he was less than two years old, after his mother died in the influenza epidemic in 1917. His own father was a dock worker who simply could not keep a job and a child. Dad was away from his home for nine miserable years, only returning when his father was planning to remarry. He left school at 14 and never went back, instead becoming an apprentice at a publishing company, and spending the rest of his life "in the print," as he called it. Despite his lack of formal education, he was one of the most avid readers and prolific letter writers I have ever met. He had beautiful, copperplate handwriting, impeccable spelling and a way of painting vivid and funny pictures with his words. He wrote what he called "doggerel," or comic verse, for the local newspaper printed by his firm, and, in his later years, even gave a major speech in rhyming couplets. He wrote more than two hundred letters to various people after Mom died, telling over and over again the story of her failed battle with cancer, as if he were trying desperately to find the reason that she had had to endure what she had endured; and perhaps to numb himself against the terrible void her illness and death had created for him. In every letter he told a little anecdote that spoke of the fun they had had together, the happy memories, silly things that they had done, or the joy of her that now lingered on in their two girls. People who received these letters laughed through their tears.

The Best Medicine and the Best Defence

Growing up, we learned that humor was a part of life; that there was a funny side to much of what we were experiencing, however bleak and miserable things might appear. But perhaps the most important lesson we learned was to laugh at ourselves; to know when to be serious, but also to know when openly recognizing one's own foibles could actually head off many a potential attack and defuse the destructive teasing. As the tallest in my class from about age 10, I knew how to respond "grow up and find out" to the perennial question "how's the weather up there?" and could always tell people how I could shut one eye and be useful as a needle in response to the taunts of "Skinny Minny" and "Bag o' Bones." The constant and anticipated jabs reached a crescendo during my high school years, when my best friend and doubles partner Sandy remained a cute, vivacious and pert 4' 11" (she *still* maintains she is 5') to my 5' 10". It is not that they didn't hurt. They did, and occasionally still do. But I had learned that to laugh at them myself, before others had the chance, was by far the best antidote.

As an adult, and particularly in my professional life, I have frequently met families whose senses of humor seem to have been mislaid. I have also met people who appear to be genetically humorless. Sometimes this is temporary, because of a transient trauma or significant depression; sometimes it seems to be part of an individual's personality. I have learned that to find a spark of humor in a child makes for almost instant rapport and that rediscovering that spark is often one of the goals in therapy with many angry, depressed or anxious individuals, children and adults alike, and within malfunctioning families. Countless difficult adolescents have described their favorite teacher, the one that they recall from the very early grades of school or the one with whom they had made that very significant connection in high school, as being "pretty strict, but with a good sense of humor." I have learned that parents who retain their sense of the absurd have a wonderful tool to relieve the stresses of their lives with their children, and that children with a sense of fun can, in turn, remind grim and intense adults that there can be a silver lining to even the darkest cloud.

As parents, we often take our jobs very seriously, especially with our first-born, and sometimes even suffer from "analysis paralysis"—inspecting and re-inspecting every aspect of what we do under a microscope, as if not taking everything seriously is a crime against our children. This is not for a moment intended to imply that being a parent is NOT a serious responsibility; of course it is. As always, the hardest part of parenting is deciding where the line is, determining whether this particular situation is one to analyze or one to laugh off. However, it is often said that laughter is the best medicine and a phenomenal stress reliever, even if things seem very serious at the time, so that attempting to find something humorous about each situation may turn out to be an important and constructive use of energy, even if the humor is at our own expense.

Copyright © 1998 by Baby Blues Partnership. Reprinted by special permission of King Features Syndicate.

Home and School: The Social Test Tubes

Home is somewhere to practice for the real world outside. As parents, we can teach our children to recognize and use humor in positive ways. The red-headed child who hears the nickname "Carrots" for the very first time in kindergarten may be less well-equipped to deal with teasing than the child who has already been exposed to it at home. As long as parents protect a child from put-downs and other forms of abuse, she can be encouraged within the family to develop an armory of verbal and non-verbal responses to deal with both the inevitable and the unexpected. Children who are overweight are the most likely to need to learn mechanisms to deal with unkind remarks, that are often superficially funny to others, but which cut deep. There is a huge and important difference between being teased about an aspect of ourselves that we can do something about, such as a habit or speech mannerism, and some characteristic with which we are saddled for life, such as shortness, large ears or other physical attributes — or, before we can change it legally, even a name. Most of us have known at least one person saddled with a joke waiting to happen: May Day, Rose Budd, Ophelia Foot, Edwina Shoes (actually, that was Edwina Hughes, but my sister could never pronounce it properly), Sidney Fuchs. I once knew of a child who had been named Ronald McDonald and who was suffering unmercifully from teasing in Grade 4. One may have little or no understanding of why some parents pick the names that they do, and may sympathize with those stuck with last names that have only recently taken on some notoriety, double-entendre or slang meaning. It is even harder to imagine that a child would be sent out into the cruel jungle of the school yard without some idea of what might happen and some means of defence when the onslaught begins.

With a Little Help from My Friends

Complicating factors sometimes add to the problem. Children with social skills' difficulties often have language-related problems that interfere with their understanding of the subtleties of humor and with their ability to respond in like, or even appropriate, manner. There are times when home can be a therapeutic place to help them cope.

—————•—————

Christine was nine years old in Grade 4, having major difficulties both inside the classroom and out on the yard. She tended to keep herself to herself, engaging in solitary pursuits such as reading, jotting notes on paper she carried with her, exploring puddles or mounds of snow or holes in fences or bugs. The other children almost universally described her as "weird." She did not always make eye contact with them, never knew what she was supposed to do in a group game or activity, and fretted about her work, often just sitting paralyzed with anxiety. She frequently cried when the other children goaded or teased her, which just made them do it more. She had a wide range of nicknames, from the obvious to the less obvious to the downright cruel. No one wanted to be her partner or in her group, and even when teachers tried to intervene or maneuver the situation to include her, she was at best neglected, at worst actively rejected. She was not a risk taker at all, and, therefore, found all athletic pursuits very threatening. The things she was interested in made the other children laugh.

Her parents were distraught and her teachers were concerned at what they all, in their own way, described as "social difficulties." Christine herself found it difficult to verbalize or otherwise express how she felt about the situation. While she cried often at school, she actually seemed quite settled at home, especially playing with her younger brother and engaging in quiet activities of her choice, either alone or with her mom or her dad. She was, however, losing sleep, not eating well and engaging in some immature behaviors. She was a very intense, serious little girl whose lower lip trembled and whose eyes filled with tears as she talked about how other children "bugged" her all the time. As she conversed more, it became clearer that her language skills were very concrete. She did not seem to be able to read between the lines, to pick up messages from people's tone of voice or to have much understanding of metaphors. For example, if you told her it was raining cats and dogs, she expected to hear the barking. She had no notion of how to tease or be teased, in any shape or form. She had little or no idea of how to respond to an attempted joke, except to make some rare eye contact and lift her eyebrows in a confused way. In fact, it was impossible to find that spark of humor at all at first.

Meeting Christine's parents, it became a little clearer where to start and where there was unlikely to be any change. Her mother was a wonderfully warm woman with endless patience and a lilting voice that would calm the most agitated child. She had the knack of coping with all Christine's upsets and restoring her to normal, and she had bent, swayed, accommodated, translated and interpreted to make sure that the world made sense for her daughter. Her father was a grown-up

Christine, without the immature behaviors. He was a very intense man who stared off at a point in space just far enough off regular eye contact to compel listeners to look over their shoulders constantly to see what he was looking at. His life was computers and he communicated best through that medium. His own language was also quite concrete and it was necessary to ensure that what had been said had in fact been received in the same mode. It was hard to say that he had no sense of humor—because he did not really give himself many opportunities to show it—but if he had one, it was definitely quite well hidden. Christine's mother, on the other hand, had an obvious, gentle sense of fun that she shared openly with her children, receiving responses and reinforcement from her son, but primarily puzzled looks from her daughter.

She was, however, able to work at helping Christine deal with various aspects of verbal social interaction. She attended some sessions with a speech/language pathologist who was able to pinpoint the language issues involved more precisely and to teach her how to interact with Christine in a manner that would encourage the development of her repertoire of responses. She gained confidence in experimenting with some gentle teasing, and Christine worked on specific comebacks she could use when she was faced with various situations with her schoolmates. Mom and Christine read together from riddle books and acted out small "plays" with puppets and stuffed animals. They watched her favorite TV shows together and laughed together, even when Mom didn't really see what Christine found so funny. At school and at home, she was encouraged to use "worry cards" to write down her concerns. Her teacher was then able to focus her attention on her work. She was given "worry time" with the resource teacher for a few minutes every day if she needed it, and her mother was able to discuss her worries with her at a given time each evening. They found that a bedtime "worry time" was resulting in even more lost sleep, but that if the worries were dealt with earlier in the evening, right after supper, she was able to take some time to relax. She could then get to bed and to sleep with greater ease.

Rather than highlighting her problems by focusing on them, Christine's teacher was encouraged to deal with the general climate of the classroom that seemed to have a high tolerance level for verbal aggression. She told the children that "in my class we all love each other, and if we don't, we pretend we do," in addition to implementing a zero-tolerance-for-put-downs rule. Children were encouraged to engage in random acts of kindness to one another, and a wide range of prosocial behaviors (including sharing, helping others, polite manners, taking turns, waiting, and so on) were noted and verbally reinforced.

As a result of all this intervention, Christine has gradually been able to increase her positive interactions with the other children in her class. She probably will never be an outgoing party animal—she is an introverted child with a love of solitude, who, to some degree, likes being the way she is—but she has learned to make occasional jokes and to tell riddles or recite funny poems, even though she is not very good at it yet. She is also learning to laugh at herself a little, and to use these skills to be able to head off confrontations with some of her peers. She has made one good friend, another youngster in her class who shares her love of exploring puddles and looking at bugs. She actually played the Wicked Stepmother, a central character in the school's Christmas concert and a humorous role that gave her permission to accept being laughed at in public. She was an unqualified success, although no one is sure that she quite understands why. Her mother has become much more comfortable in seeking, recognizing and using humor at home to deal with all kinds of behavior and other situations, and this has been a pleasure for her. Her husband, Christine's father, is still an intense, serious fellow who misses much of what is going on around him, but, as we know, sometimes ignorance is bliss.

—•—

Lost...and Found

Humor is such a strange phenomenon. It is unique to each individual; yet it is its common elements that allow us to share laughter. Recognizing one's own sense of humor or lack thereof can be enlightening. Have I lost it or did I never have it? Humor in parenting is particularly hard to find at times. Do try to find it! Children are unbelievably funny in their quest to grow up and we have to learn to keep a straight face at the time so that they can maintain their dignity. We know that Kids Say The Darndest Things. At least other people's kids seem to, especially when they are talking to Bill Cosby. But ours do also. My sister grew up believing that the Lord's Prayer began "Our Father Who Aunty Helen..." One dad told me that his son, who had discovered reading at a very young age, announced at dinner one night, aged all of six years, that he was having trouble eating his food because "the villi in my lower intestines have not yet absorbed all the nutrients from what I ate before." When parenting becomes burdensome, read Erma Bombeck's *Motherhood: the Second Oldest Profession*. If you've read it before, read it again. Read Lynn Johnston's *For Better or For Worse* cartoon books, or Rick Kirkman and Jerry Scott's *Baby Blues* or Bill Watterson's *Calvin and Hobbes*. Rent a funny movie. Some people would tell you just to laugh; go on, laugh and keep laughing. Some studies have apparently shown that this helps. Call your mother or father and ask if they can tell you something funny that you did as a child. If they can't, at least you know how you came by your lack of a sense of humor!

Chapter 2

Everybody Else's Parents Let Them...

The "Mythical Family"

You are, I am certain, already quite familiar with the Mythical Family — if not yet, then you will be. Our children discover this family from the time they meet the world outside the home and increasingly so into adolescence when this family becomes all-consuming. This is the family where the parents are perennially benign, voices are never raised, and there are cupboards full of candy bars. The children are allowed to wear, eat, say, view or do *whatever* they wish *whenever* they wish. Nobody else's parents make them wear mitts or hats in the winter, or bicycle helmets, or dorky clothes of any kind. Everybody else's parents let them watch TV until they wish to watch no more and provide a bottomless pit of money which can be spent on designer jeans, junk food and all manner of uncensored extra-curricular activities. These same parents provide endless hours of patient support with homework, but, of course, they never *make* their children work if the children prefer to play or watch TV. They do not make their children eat disgusting food, nor do they expect them to help out around the house. They drive their children anywhere they wish to go at all times and never complain. They do not have dumb rules like curfews, and they are their children's memories, so that field trips are never missed, lunch is always at school when required, and homework is always completed on time. They never nag about keeping rooms tidy, or anything else for that matter. In fact, they don't put on any pressure at all.

In reality, our children will meet friends whose parents sometimes do some of these things. If we are honest, we will recognize that we do some of these things some of the time, so that we open the door to the possibility that we could perhaps be like this all the time. Thus is born the prototype family from which our children build their ideal. These parents behave like this to their children, our children tell us, so that their children will always be happy and appreciative. "Just wait until *you* have children—*then* you'll understand!" we tell them. But we worry. We ruminate about whether we are being mean, and whether we are doing the "right thing." Occasionally we even give in under the pressures of cross-examination and against our better judgment and try to behave like this "mythical family," so that our children will be happy and we can feel appreciated.

A Good Look at Ourselves

Most myths grow from a small seed of truth. They can, therefore, provide some occasional, useful opportunities for self-evaluation. The following story illustrates different perspectives on everybody else's family and how looking around us can be quite helpful, for parents as well as for children.

———•———

Yvonne sought help, as she had many times previously, for assistance with parenting her three children, aged 10 to 16. She wanted to find out what they had been doing wrong and why their family was, to use Yvonne's words, "so dysfunctional." The 14-year-old was being defiant and non-compliant, totally on strike around the house and only interested in spending time with her friends, either in person or on the telephone, at all hours of the day and night. The 16-year-old had had some difficult times earlier in her teens, but was now quite independent, and they saw little of her, what with her part-time job, her boyfriend and her skating. Yvonne wanted to make sure she did things "right" with the youngest before it was "too late."

Yvonne and David had met in high school and had been married for many years, with neither ever really dating anyone else even half seriously before they were engaged. She quit her job as a teacher when their first child was born and had remained an at-home mother ever since, filling her time volunteering at the local schools, running Brownie and Guide packs, chairing the fundraising committee for the skating club, and various other activities that kept her fully involved with her children's lives. David had initially been quite supportive of full-time motherhood, but had gradually found himself somewhat dispensable. He frequently felt downright incompetent when he tried to regain some of his parental role with the children. As a consequence, he had retreated into his career and his golf, although he retained a close relationship with all three children, more as a confidant and buddy than as a parent. They would often go to him with complaints about Mom's rules and regulations and he vainly attempted to mediate and negotiate. The result was an unhappy dad, who felt left out of his parenting role, and an unhappy mom, who felt overburdened, unsupported, perennially the "bad cop." Frequently, she felt as if she had four children, instead of just three.

When she explored her own family background, it became evident that, unlike most of us, she had not discovered the Mythical Family during her childhood, believing instead that the way her family functioned was the only way families were and, therefore, that it was normal. It was not until her adult years that this "other family" had not only been unearthed, but had also become something of an obsession.

Yvonne was herself the oldest of three children. She had two younger brothers, and, as long as she could remember, she had been a mother. She had taken care of most of the housework and cooking, and had looked after the boys with all the energy she could muster. This, she thought, was what her mother expected her to do. She thought her dad had similar expectations, but she always felt she did not really know him very well. He was a physician whose patients always took priority and who spent a lot of time behind his study door whenever he was home. When she had not been very good at mothering and the younger children had not done as they were supposed to do, her mother had sighed and told her that it was fine, the boys were a real handful; but Yvonne had always known that she should have done better. She became very irritated with her brothers who always seemed to delight in her misery, and she retained some of this resentment to this day. Her mother had also been a stay-at-home mother, but seemed to spend all her time sick in bed, or tired, or irritable, or simply not there. Yvonne had always tried to make her mother feel better, but nothing seemed to work. Yvonne had had no life outside home except for school, where she had excelled. Report card time was the only time that she felt she was pleasing her parents. They were SO proud of her, they told her. She had met David in high school, but they had waited until she had finished teachers' college before they married.

It was while she was at college that she first realized that not all families were like hers. David's family, for example, was quite different. They were loud and huggy and generous, and the family home was a disastrous contrast to Yvonne's notions of peace and quiet. His mother had worked all her life and yet seemed to do everything around the house as well, pretty much waiting hand and foot on her husband and her boys. Although Yvonne had always known it at some level, it was becoming more obvious to her that her friends had also had quite different upbringings. They had been children. They had not had to spend all their time looking after the house or keeping the little ones quiet so that Dad could do his work. They had not had to be mothers to their mother. They had married ambitious men who seemed to do everything from coaching little league to helping out in the senior citizens' home. In the parts she listened to, they were always talking about their children who appeared to be universally successful in and out of school. Gradually but inexorably, Yvonne painted her own picture of the Mythical Family.

In her Mythical Family, the mother was perfect. She was totally competent and looked after everyone all the time. She was responsible for the smooth running of the household and the health and well-being of all its occupants. In her Mythical Family, even though its members had chosen traditional roles, the husband helped out at home even before he was asked. He anticipated the mother's every whim. He intervened at precisely the right moment, heading off all confrontations with just a tiny injection of support for her well-laid plans. The Mythical Children were, of course, all obedient and loving, achieving well in school and active in all forms of extra-curricular activities. They much preferred spending time with the family, rather than off with their friends, although, of course, they struck an excellent balance so that they were socially popular and adept. They instinctively knew right from wrong, responded the very first time their parents made even the most modest request, adored their siblings and ate only healthy food in appropriate quantities, automatically clearing their dishes before retreating to their impeccably kept rooms to do their homework—without being reminded, of course.

It is obvious to all of us that this notion of the Mythical Family was bound to make Yvonne feel worthless—and, of course, it did. Not only did her husband and children not live up to her expectations, which disappointed and discouraged her, but she failed miserably to live up to her own, which depressed her. On the one hand, when she took a closer, more rational look at the Mythical Family, she was able to see and, eventually, to understand that the way that she had been brought up had registered within her a number of messages about who she was and what her mission in life was. She began to realize that what she had taken as "normal" was perhaps not what most people had experienced. This realization made her very sad and she needed to take some time to grieve the loss of the family life and the childhood that she would have liked to have had. She was also able to see that it was possible to be different from her own mother and to make life for her children quite different from what her own had been. She gradually realized that her expectations for everyone, including herself, were unrealistic and bound to produce disappointment. Not only did she feel incompetent because she was unable to live up to them, but David and the children also felt inadequate. It took a great deal of effort and courage for her to relinquish her ideal, but she was able to create a role for herself as a mother that allowed some human frailties, and permitted the other family members to take on increasing levels of responsibility, however imperfect their initial attempts might be. In the process, she found a renewed sense of intimacy with David as they became partners in parenting, since he proved to be quite supportive, creative and innovative, when she let him be. She also unearthed a spark of humor as they watched the ways the children reacted to the new world in which they lived. After joining a parent support group, she discovered that her teens were actually quite normal and that her family, far from being dysfunctional, was actually quite together. In fact, she quit the group, finished with therapy and rejoined the world—still occasionally yearning for the Mythical Family and still feeling somewhat disappointed when it didn't materialize, but generally much more content in her current reality.

—•—

Navel-Gazing

One of the main factors that causes us to crumble under pressure is that, as parents, we get virtually no feedback about the job we are doing. For the most part, parents are highly motivated to do a good job raising their children. The problem is that most of us cannot really define the job, and even when we can, we cannot actually measure whether what we are doing is working. What do we look at in order to evaluate our performance?

Primarily, we tend to look to our children's behavior and general sense of well-being. If they are well-behaved and happy, we can be pretty sure we are doing a good job. Since normal children spend some of their time being well-behaved and happy, many of us are reasonably content for part of the time. However, like nervous exam candidates, we tend to focus on what we don't know or what we did wrong, and discount all the good stuff. Therefore, we take small examples of inappropriate behavior or the odd spell of unhappiness and assume that we are failing the grade. Especially for our first child.

Sometimes we have the confidence to use other people's children as a yardstick for measuring our own children's behavior and judging our own performance as parents. Unfortunately, just like Yvonne, we all seem to know the equivalent of the Mythical Family with whom our children are so familiar. We know that Other People's Children seem to be clean and well-behaved in church; they say "please" and "thank you" without being reminded through gritted teeth. They do as they are told without being spoken to twice. When they are little, they never want to watch TV because they spend all day making creative objects with recyclable materials and macaroni. As they get older, they do their homework and go to bed without being asked. As adolescents, they keep their rooms comfortably tidy; and they hang out only with acceptable friends whose faces and bodies are relatively unmutilated. They are content to help out around the house in addition to getting good marks

PEANUTS reprinted by permission of United Feature Syndicate, Inc.

and having their choice of part-time jobs, university programs and functional relationships. In the face of these criteria, how can we ever compete?

Fortunately, just as our children meet parents they would rather not live with, we also meet children who make ours look good. Thus, the myth of the Mythical Family is perpetuated and reinforced!

Parental Report Cards

Another common source of evaluation for parents is, of course, our child's report card. This is partly why we are so insistent on whipping it out of his hand or his school bag and looking immediately at the comments and the part that relates to the non-academic skills such as "plays well with others," "shares," and other euphemisms for "has been well brought up." I have often wondered whether kindergarten teachers realize that they are actually evaluating our parenting, and not our children.

The approval or disapproval of our own parents and significant others provides a powerful, if occasionally suspect, yardstick by which to measure our performance. Caring what other people think is a major tool of socialization that serves to tame the wild savage born inside all of us. Abiding by the rules of society in varying degrees is what makes us civilized human beings. However, change is inevitable, particularly from generation to generation. Without it, society would stagnate. Change for the sake of change is, however, sometimes counterproductive.

Goal-Setting for Self-Esteem

As we shall explore later, the most important way to evaluate our parental performance is to set some goals for what we wish to achieve in raising our children, and then to evaluate our performance based on those goals. If we can establish that they are reasonable and realistic, and that the results they produce are socially and humanistically acceptable, they form a valid basis upon which to build. Then we can revisit them occasionally to determine if we are on track or not. We can fine tune various aspects of what we are doing, collect input from various sources, and generally keep expectations in line with what we can reasonably produce. We can then accept or reject the information we receive from our observations of others and create our own family mosaic as we want it to be.

The Two-Way Street

We know only too well that parenting is not something you simply do TO a child. We know that we can do exactly the same thing to the same child on two different occasions and produce two different results. We also know that we can do something that works well with one of our children and not with the others. Yet further, we know that the result of what we do will affect how we act on subsequent occasions; so we actually change what we do, depending on the outcome. One of the basic rules of parenting, indeed, of life, seems to be: if it works, do it again; if it doesn't work, make sure it was set up properly and try it one more time; if it still doesn't work, go back to the drawing board and try something different. We need to remain aware that our perceptions are the reality by which we live and make decisions. Therefore we need to check our perceptions against realities other than our own from time to time. This can serve as validation for our perspectives, or it can provide us with alternatives from which to choose. Set goals—short-term, medium-term, long-term—for yourself as a person and as a parent, and see how you're doing. Adjust the goals so that you can achieve success. When we are depressed, deciding to get out of bed is a perfectly valid goal; once we have achieved that, we can then decide to get up and get dressed. This is the way that success is born. On such small successes self-esteem can grow, even self-esteem as a parent. Learn to use the phrases: "Consider the source," "I am NOT everybody else's mother," "And in OUR family we…," and "Send me a postcard when you get there so I can come and live there too." Remember that, to others, YOU are everybody else's family.

Chapter 3

Surely This Can't Be Normal!

Universals—and Individual Differences

As parents, especially first-time parents, we tend to think that whatever our child is doing at any given time will probably go on for ever: waking in the night whimpering for food or comfort; needing four books read from cover to cover before shutting an eyelid to sleep; taking antibiotics for ear infections; having screaming temper tantrums; calling "shotgun!" every time before getting into the car. We yearn to hear the phrase: "It's only a phase," especially when those sweet words come from a pediatrician or our mother-in-law. We can then truly believe that this, too, will pass.

Fortunately, most children do grow out of most things. Not too many young adults are in training pants, sucking on a pacifier, for example. The vast majority of children are eating solid food by the time they get to kindergarten. And grown men shower. When we look at the universals of development—those stages of childhood that seem to occur in precisely the same order and manner whether a child is born in downtown Montreal or in the jungles of Indonesia—we realize that all children are programmed to babble before they speak in words, to sit before they walk, to flail around with their hands before they can pick up tiny crumbs in their fingers. In other words, a preset plan is simply there for the unfolding and, in the absence of trauma to the system, will evolve in the natural course of events. Decades of research have shown that a child's environment plays a huge role in shaping both personality and behavior, but the influences of preprogrammed genetics, including universal developmental patterns, remain strong. We have also discovered that children are born with certain predispositions to interact with their world in predictable ways. As any parent of more than one child knows, children are born with different temperaments. Our three pregnancies were as different from each other as our children turned out to be. Some children are wired to be awkward, other to be placid, still others to be curious and active learners. Their innate differences, along with our reactions to those differences, will shape and form the path of our interactions for as long as we are involved with each other.

Cuddlers and Non-Cuddlers

Some patterns of behavior that are present from birth have deep and significant impacts on how we see ourselves as parents. Cuddlers and non-cuddlers, for example, exist in almost equivalent proportions in the general population of infants, the latter being defined not by their capacity for affection but by their rejection of restraint. They hate to be confined, even if the confinement is in the arms of a loving parent and even if they are beside themselves with fatigue. They wriggle and arch, struggle to get down from our laps, and simply do not mold to our bodies. Even such a deceptively simple characteristic can result in very different parent-child relationships. For a first-time mom who picks up a fretful baby with the expectation that she will settle and calm, the sense of rejection she feels when that same baby frantically fights being held, rocked and nursed can be devastating; and the feelings of parental incompetence are born. First-time moms and dads assume that it is something about *them*—that there is something they are not doing right—or that there is something very wrong with the baby. In such circumstances, parents are torn. They want to hold and comfort the child, but they realize that the child does not seem to need their touch. They may persist with picking up and holding the baby, only to increase the struggles, or they may abandon the idea and resort to "distance" parenting by putting the baby in her crib and communicating from afar. They may, on the odd occasion, just leave the baby to settle herself. In extreme cases, they may stop trying. Females tend, whether through biology or sociology, to pick up, hold and snuggle with babies, whereas males tend to engage in play-type behaviors that are physically more active. Thus, non-cuddlers and their moms may have a more difficult time than non-cuddlers and their dads.

When a first-born child is a cuddler, this is what parents expect. Therefore, their perceptions of that baby may well be more positively oriented. It is when the *second* child is a non-cuddler that the attributions of "fault" begin to appear. That second child is more likely to be looked upon as "difficult" than the parents are to question their own parenting strategies.

Is this a phase? Will the child outgrow this tendency all by herself? As children get older, they sometimes change. A warm, affectionate, cuddly pre-teen becomes cool and distant as he struggles to separate from his child-self. A squirming, active, leave-me-be youngster turns into a young adult who snuggles beside you on the couch as you try to read the paper or watch TV. Certainly, most children will go through periods where they fight intensely for their independence and autonomy from their parents. If a child has been a non-cuddler, this quest does not come as a surprise. Parents are less likely to interpret it as a "phase" and more likely to see it as the child's continuing journey into life. If a child has, however, always been a close, affectionate youngster who has depended heavily on adult support, it is more palatable to think of the forays into independence as "phases" that will soon go away.

This, Too, Shall Pass—or Will It?

The manifestation of certain behaviors because of given developmental needs and particular environmental factors will clearly result in "phases." These phases can be positive or negative. Many young children go through a wonderful phase where they think that everything we do as parents is awesome. I can remember asking our young son when he was in a particularly loving and affectionate period of his life to promise me that he would be like this for ever. Unfortunately, this type of phase seems to disappear all by itself, even though we try hard to hang on to it and reinforce it with every breath in our bodies! Negative behaviors, it seems, do not always have the same magical way of disappearing.

Temper tantrums are one type of behavior that parents fervently hope

© Lynn Johnston Productions Inc./Distributed by United Feature Syndicate, Inc.

constitute a phase. Tantrums are normal, until we have learned other, more socially-acceptable ways to express our feelings. For many children, the temper phase begins around the age of two—"the Terrible Twos"—and lasts until the child's ability to use words takes over and the world is once again understandable and, to some degree, controllable. For children who bypass the Terrible Twos, this "phase" often hits at four or five or, perhaps, in the teen years. Few of us manage to avoid it completely. However, children need assistance to develop their competence with words, whether they are two, five or 12. Just leaving them to rant and rave, or punishing this behavior, will not usually teach them more adaptive strategies to use in the face of frustration.

——•——

Trevor was 13 and having a terrible time at home. He was an only child who lived primarily with Nancy, his mom. She was finding it impossible to get him to do anything she wanted him to do. He would yell and scream, pout, sulk, slam doors, punch holes in walls, break things. He had recently begun to threaten her physically, although he had not actually touched her—yet. These behaviors were often triggered by simple requests or comments, such as "and how was your day?" or "it's time for supper." It was a particularly scary incident that involved some violence on HER part that brought her to seek some help for herself. She hated the fact that she had once actually grabbed him and slapped him across the face when he had been screaming obscenities at her for not letting him do some now-forgotten activity. Everywhere else Trevor went, people said what a lovely boy he was. Therefore, she was absolutely convinced the problem was with her and so was far

——•——

more concerned about what she had done than about anything that Trevor had done or was still doing. However, there had been a couple of calls from the school lately. A teacher who liked Trevor a lot was concerned at some changes he had noticed in the boy's behavior and said he had the impression that Trevor was quite an angry young man. Nancy had been disturbed by the call, but was quite definite in her perception that Trevor's behavior was normal for a teenager, especially a boy who did not have a father's influence in the house. Wasn't it? And she was convinced that he was in a "phase" that would eventually just blow over. Wouldn't it? Her concern was simply how she could outlast it.

When he saw his dad every second weekend, Trevor was reportedly fine. They went to his hockey games, scoured the wreckers' yards for parts for the old car they were fixing up, and spent the rest of the time watching sports on TV and entertaining his friends. Trevor loved going and hated leaving. His parents had been separated since he was four years old and he had very little, if any, memory of his life in the intact family. Both his parents had had a series of relationships and Trevor had really liked a couple of these people. He had stopped trying to attach to any of them, however, because he never knew whether they would be there the next week. He had become a little gun-shy. You could be disappointed only so often.

According to Nancy's recollection, he had started having temper tantrums when he was about four years old. At the time, she put it down to the separation and the fact that she and Trevor's dad had been fighting openly both before and after they had parted ways. There had been much dissent over where Trevor would live, for how long and who should take him where, when, and all the other issues that befall so very many children in this situation. He had reacted by screaming, ranting and raving whenever he was with his mom. He frequently yelled that he hated her, that he wished she were dead, that he just wanted his dad back and that he wanted to know why she had sent him away. Nancy was completely devastated by the extent of his anger. She felt very guilty that the marriage had broken up. Despite all the hostility and fighting, it had taken her and her ex three agonizing years to decide that it was really over between them. Thus, to hear all her doubts and guilts expressed by her four-year-old was just too much. She sympathized with him and took his punishment for as long as she could stand it. Then she blew up, put him in his room and tried to wait it out. Then she would feel bad, apologize, and let him start again. By the time he was six, Trevor was informing her that it was her fault Dad had left. The message was clear that she had better make it up to him…or else. She tried everything she could to appease him. She tried explaining why she did what she did, and tried persuading him to agree with her that what she did was a really good idea. She actually did have good reasons, but Trevor wasn't convinced, and kept insisting on having things his way. He was getting more and more desperate. By the time he was eight, he was trashing his room, and by 10 was punching holes in the drywall. By 12, he was screaming obscenities, and now, at 13, he was taller and heavier than Nancy and becoming physically intimidating.

This was no phase that would pass on its own. It was clear that Trevor's behavior had to be dealt with, or he would become even more of a danger to himself and to others. The longer it was left, the more difficult it would become. He and Nancy were in a high-risk, potentially abusive relationship that could result in serious violence to either one of them. It was also pretty clear that trying to persuade him that it was a good idea to stop would not cut too much mustard. He had some deep-seated anger because of the separation, an almost universal anger which some separated or divorced parents, Nancy included, feel (or wish) children should have overcome and dealt with so many years after the fact. Trevor, like so many children, had not dealt with it. Neither did he want to. He wasn't the one asking for help.

As she reviewed his behavioral history, Nancy decided that, although the behavior may have changed, the general pattern had not. She realized that she had felt sorry for him and that her busy life and her own pain, after the marriage failed, had stopped her following through on plans for handling Trevor and his tantrums. This "phase" had, in effect, lasted nine years and showed no signs of abating. In fact it was escalating. Something had to be done. First, both Nancy and Trevor had to deal with the issue of separating his feelings from his behavior, so that each could be handled individually. Once Trevor's feelings of anger, frustration, resentment and anxiety could be identified, they could be listened to and acknowledged. Since he was not the least interested in counseling, Nancy was the only one with a chance to do that listening. This was difficult because she was indeed the target for at least some of his negative feelings. She talked about how resentful SHE was that her ex-husband did not get any of the flak that she put up with, but was able to see the up and the down side of the fact that Trevor was not at all comfortable expressing his anger to his dad: his dad wouldn't put up with it and he was afraid his dad would disappear. It was cold comfort to Nancy to realize that she was a safer target for Trevor's feelings.

She gradually become more comfortable with allowing Trevor to feel what he felt, but was able to place much firmer limits on what he was permitted to do with those feelings. She provided a time for him to talk them through, if he chose. This he occasionally did once he began to trust her to listen, although he wasn't really a "talk-it-out" kind of guy. She and Trevor came up with some absolutely non-negotiable limits in terms of violence (i.e., none) and other abusive behaviors (e.g., obscenities, put-downs, vandalism) that applied to them both. Once zero tolerance for any of these was established, it was no longer necessary to engage in long debates to determine whether or not a particular behavior was an exception to the rule. There were no exceptions. They agreed on a range of behaviors that would be acceptable when he was angry. This was difficult because he had a real need to be physical in his rage, but they could agree on his pounding an old work bench in the basement with a rubber mallet, and ripping up old telephone books. These wouldn't hurt anyone and they made him feel better. Although it was hard for her, Nancy agreed to let him retreat to his room if he felt he needed time out. She promised not to pursue him. He made the same agreement for her. He was also allowed to stomp, to close his door firmly and to raise his voice, provided it didn't break any of the non-negotiable rules. It was Trevor's job to repair any damage. Once the damage was repaired, his life was pretty much back to normal. If his activities were restricted because he had not paid his dues or done his community service, this was his choice, not Nancy's. It took Nancy a while to realize that this was a way for Trevor to learn to take more responsibility for his own behavior and that she did not have to feel guilty about this. Most importantly, Nancy was able to take a little time to explore her own responses to Trevor's behavior. She realized that they were rooted in her own past history, and that she was a major role model for how he would learn to treat the women of the world, including potential girlfriends and mates. Interestingly, she was more willing to stand up for the rest of us than she had been to stand up for herself. If she had had the money, the time and the inclination, some ongoing therapy might have been of additional help. But she had none of these. Trevor's behavior had started to settle down and she was beginning to feel more in control of her own life and happiness. She had recently met a "nice, warm guy" who really liked Trevor and who made her feel good about herself. Life could still be beautiful.

If It's Broke, Try to Fix It

Some mandatory education in child development would no doubt be introduced if ever we had to pass a certification program before we became parents. In the absence of even the remotest possibility that this will happen, it seems it's up to us to educate ourselves. In my day, we read Dr. Benjamin Spock and T. Berry Brazelton; the subsequent generation ran to Penelope Leach. They all bridge the generational gap in providing information on basic child development; what is normal when, where, how and why. Brazelton always suited my taste because he allowed for children with different temperaments, and I could always find myself and my children inside his pages. But we all have our own favorites. Making use of "management consultants"—our parents, in-laws, relatives, friends and professionals—can also fill a void. Regardless of our sources, we must make sure we can find information when we need it, and, even more, know when to stop looking and get on with things.

Finding strategies for changing a child's behavior is an ongoing task for parents, and no one has yet written, or ever will write, the definitive book on exactly how to do it. This is because of the myriad of individual differences and the unique set of interactions between personalities in every single parent-child relationship that result in a different mosaic for each and every child produced, even to the same parents. However broad the range of behaviors that are considered "normal," one's own tolerance levels are important sensors in determining when there is a problem in a family. In some families, a sore finger is a major problem; in others, family violence is a way of life. If we are concerned that particular behaviors may, in fact, not be simply a phase, but a problem, we need to feel comfortable checking this out with someone whom we trust and whom we feel will not judge us for asking. Some of us are lucky and have a lot of resources either within our extended families or beyond; others are very much alone. Family doctors are often a good start because they are accessible to most people; priests, ministers and rabbis are also frequently easy to find. However, professionals who are judgmental are not only unhelpful but can be harmful, so we also have to get our acts together if we are to be useful resources.

Parenting conferences and workshops can provide an anonymous forum for asking questions and receiving reassurance; and books of all kinds, hopefully including this one, can supply an overwhelming range of insights, strategies and ideas.

Remember also that there are many different "phases" in parenting. You'll simply outgrow some of them.

In the meantime, we can try to plan what we would like to do as parents. As Virginia Satir says, we can be the "architects" of the family, and we can make good use of flexibility in terms of refining the plans as we go along, to make our design adaptable and functional in the real world. However, we need a vision of what we are trying to build, and we need to set goals that are in line with that vision if we are ever to feel that we are succeeding.

Chapter 4

Motherhood, Fatherhood, Parenthood

Maternal Instinct: The Philosopher's Stone of Parenthood

Before we had children, I thought that maternal instinct would just appear on the scene as part of the delivery process. Wasn't it some magic feeling that washed over new mothers as they gazed at their newborn offspring? I hoped so. I had never really had much to do with babies up to and including the time I was overcome with the mystifying but overwhelming urge to produce one. At the time, it seemed a very natural thing to do, although some of our friends were trying to come up with good reasons for starting a family and failing to do so. During the pregnancy there were certainly stirrings of something very biological. We were both awed by the presence of an unknown, already-loved third person in our relatively new relationship. If my husband could have physically carried his share of the pregnancy, he certainly would have; he most definitely carried it emotionally. We both celebrated the first fluttering movements, both listened to the gurgles and felt the elbows and knees, and both counted down the days and eventually the contractions. We both had the instinct—and we knew it.

It was quite an eye-opener when I returned home from the hospital with our firstborn daughter. In those days in the early '70s, new mothers could stay up to five days in the hospital, being coddled by nursery-ward nurses to make sure you thought you knew what you were doing before you strutted your stuff in the real world. I should have known better. Before giving birth to our breathtakingly beautiful, no-neck-no-nose, black-lashed, black-eyed, black-haired little girl, it turned out that I knew basically two things. Firstly,

I had learned over many hours of instruction and practice how to breathe during fake childbirth. Secondly, I knew how to bathe a doll. Once the profoundly moving experience of birth had taken place, and before leaving the sanctuary of the hospital, I found out that I knew diddly.

For a start, I had discovered that breathing deeply was physically impossible when you were holding your breath in excruciating pain, and that it was, in any case, useful only to swear loudly at the very nice people who were desperately trying to encourage you to breathe deeply. In addition, I had found out that fake childbirth did not hold a candle to the real thing and that I was surely no martyr when it came to tolerating true pain. Finally, I now also knew that there was a whole, vast universe of difference between firmly grasping a rubber arm under the prescient eye of our prenatal coach, while washing a compliant doll-body all over, and trying to hang on to a slippery, wriggling, infuriated, seven-pound baby, who was threatening to drown herself if I so much as blinked. Thus, all that I thought I knew was instantaneously wiped out and I found myself starting with a clean slate. Within those first few days, my learning curve was steep, fueled by the overwhelming sense of responsibility that had entered my world the moment my husband reluctantly returned to the predictability of work. I waited for instinct to wash over me and tell me what to do.

My main lesson has stayed with me ever since. Maternal instinct, if present at all, did not appear to be very useful.

There was never any question that I was very firmly attached to our babies. So was my husband. In fact, I think we had bonded at about Week 2 of pregnancy, just around the time the little strip changed to the right color. In fact, all our pregnancies were very important bonding times for us. This has helped me in my work to understand and to share the grief of many mothers who have miscarried or aborted, even within the first few weeks, and who mourn the loss of that child-to-be. Even in those first few weeks after conception, I knew that there was going to be no separating us. By the time each baby was born, I could not have been more bonded. We were joined at the hip, yea, velcroed together, and the thought of the gazillion dangers that threatened this little, vulnerable part of me in the real world was sufficient to trigger those signs of anxiety deep down inside that were to become more familiar over the ensuing years. Without question, I knew immediately and instinctively that I would do whatever I had to do to take care of our children, that I would throttle with my bare hands anyone who threatened them with harm and that, if anything happened to them, I would quite willingly die. I still know this. This may be wonderful insight and a profound, almost religious, experience. It may be love. Unfortunately, it has its limitations when it comes to the day-to-day function of being a mother.

Several interesting thoughts came to mind as I waited for instinct to wash over me. It struck me forcefully how much more instinctive my husband was than I, and he has remained so throughout our child-raising years. I have never ONCE caught him with a baby in one arm and a child-rearing book in his other hand. Nor have I heard him bawling his eyes out in the middle of the night wailing that he had "fed her, and changed her and she's still crying and I don't know what to do." He has always seemed to know what to do for a fever, or how to calm a frantic toddler, or even how to keep a child amused for more than five minutes without a TV. He can stand doing homework with teenagers who know everything already. He has nurtured and protected, kept his children safe, loved them deeply, and even more deeply grieved the end of their childhood. And all this from an engineer! I continue to envy him this ease and confidence. And here am I, a child psychologist, studying child development during the very same years that I was becoming a mother, setting myself up to help other mothers and fathers and children and families, and yet still a quivering mass of indecision, second-guessing and failed attempts at mastering this supposedly instinctive job.

Who Needs Instinct?

If it weren't for the instinct to procreate, there would probably be zero population growth, although some people may be able to think up some logical reasons for having children. Such an instinct to have babies is in most cases strong enough to overcome memories of the most nerve-wracking physical pain most of us will ever feel. In fact, even before we have experienced it, people (not only men, but also other women) are telling us not to worry because we will forget it sooner or later. There was a recent news report of a woman who sued the doctors who delivered her twins because they failed to make her childbirth pain-free. The responses of women in general were quite remarkable. In a nutshell, they could be summed up as *"What?* We all had to suffer and we are all grateful, and we got on with having babies anyhow"—or something along those lines. Evidently, the instinct to breed does not separate us by much of a margin from either our evolutionary predecessors or your common-or-garden rabbits. There are baby-booms after every war; nature's way of catching up. Maternal instinct, when defined as the instinct to procreate, has to be related to the long-term survival of the species; as such it is alive and well.

A more serious advantage of maternal instinct in its more general definition is obviously related to the need to protect the young of the species and to provide a nurturing environment in which the youngsters can grow from utter helplessness to the point of complete independence. Someone presumably has to *want* to do this. Because women have traditionally been the stay-with-the-baby parent, and because they are innately equipped as a source of food, they have been expected to provide this nurturing and protective environment for children; in other words, to possess the instinct to mother.

But is mothering a gender issue? Some classic research studies looking at baby monkeys reared apart from their natural mothers showed that they attached themselves firmly to a genderless "surrogate" figure that was soft and cuddly, rather than to a wire figure, regardless of which figure provided them with food. Other studies of young ducklings found that they "imprinted" upon whomever was in their environment, and spent hours following white-coated scientists in a manner reminiscent of the rats following the Pied Piper. Thus, the "instinct" of attachment or bonding, while most likely to be between the primary caregiver and the infant, does not appear to be exclusive to females. It has been demonstrated that males are equally capable of becoming attached to their infants, given the opportunity.

Is Motherhood a Gender Issue?

A number of years ago, Letty Cottin Pogrebin (*Growing Up Free*) wrote from a feminist perspective about the dangers of believing in maternal instinct. Her views can be summarized as follows.

- The myth of maternal instinct implies that it is easy to be a good mother, coming naturally as it does, and therefore that any woman can do it. If you can't, you must be a failure. This, Ms Pogrebin says, is the "wellspring of mother-guilt for all women."

- Society undervalues motherhood because it is seen as instinctive and not requiring real skills. Mother substitutes (e.g., child-care workers, teachers, nurses) have, therefore, been traditionally underpaid. We know that staying home to raise children is not considered to be an "occupation" worth even income tax relief, let alone some recognition of value, although *Dear Abby*, in 1989, calculated the monetary equivalent of the services provided by a full-time mother to be $52,000 (US) per year.

- The instinct to be a mother is so strong that it is not worth training or hiring females in top-level positions because they will "just get pregnant and leave." Hopefully, this is changing because of intense lobbying by various women's organizations, but the kernel of doubt frequently remains. Women must still choose between maintaining their career paths and taking time out to do the most important job they will ever have.

- Women are becoming "herded" into full and exclusive responsibility for children. "Father is the volunteer parent, the back-up man. Lacking 'the instinct,' everything he does is a miracle or a favor…. When fathers care for their own children, mothers are supposed to be impressed and grateful."

This approach espouses the political view that it is very convenient for males to keep women as the primary caregivers so that they can "keep the power" and "keep control over the next generation without having to get involved until children are older, more civilized and more rewarding." Men are then, apparently, forced to repress their love for their babies as "unnatural and unmanly" and, thus, remain distanced from their children, even though there is evidence to support the notion that adult males are as attracted to babies as adult females—provided the conditions are non-ego-threatening!

Psychological research over the past 50 years or so supports the notion that males are quite capable of bonding with and caring for their children. Studies on animals reveal that, when forced to live with infants in the absence of their mates, male primates rear the infants competently. In general, however, despite the *ability* to be active, nurturing, involved caregivers with their infants, in many instances, fathers choose not to follow this pattern. Society does not consider them inadequate because of this. However, women who choose not to be active, nurturing, involved caregivers are almost uniformly seen as suspect—less by men, perhaps, than by other women.

Letty Cottin Pogrebin concludes that we should argue away the premise of innate behavior, get rid of the "motherhood mandate" and start from scratch with the following rules of thumb:

- To learn about motherhood, don't ask a sociobiologist, ask a mother (or read one of the honest books written by mothers about their feelings and experiences).
- Not all women are meant to be mothers, and no individual woman is meant to be only a mother and nothing else.
- Two parents want a child. Two parents make a child. Two parents raise a child. Neither parent was born knowing how to do it. Both parents can learn.

There is little doubt that some fathers possess more parenting instinct than some mothers. There is less doubt that many fathers are given, or in fact may take, little opportunity to become significant figures in their children's lives. And there is no doubt that children benefit from having both parents actively involved in their upbringing, instinct or no instinct.

Copyright © 1998 by Baby Blues Partnership. Reprinted by special permission of King Features Syndicate.

The Dark Side of the Force

A less obvious aspect of instinct occurs to a number of mothers, including myself, during those first few weeks and months of motherhood. There is a dark side to maternal instinct that each of us believes to be unique to herself. It is the other end of the extreme feelings dimension, from extreme, intense love and wonder at one end, to extreme, intense rage, perhaps based in deep anxiety, at the other. It is frightening how frustrated we can become with a helpless infant. We are scared by her total dependence on us and her inability to tell us what is wrong. We feel desperately incompetent to meet her needs, especially when something as natural as breastfeeding that is supposed to be so instinctive, and that is so satisfying when it goes well, seems to be doing little for her satisfaction. In fact, everything we eat seems to disagree with her, and she appears to be constantly hungry. She does not quiet down when we try to hold her and rock her. She fights sleep and seems to writhe in some hidden pain. We are told "she is colicky." The effects of night after night of sleep deprivation begin to take their toll on us, and we start to wonder what all this is for. The demands of others, other children, spouse, the world at large, await at the threshold of the bedroom door. We rail, we rage, we despair. We sometimes come terrifyingly close to acting on our negative feelings. Yet we are shocked to hear of others who do.

When I was at this stage with our firstborn, I was deeply affected by a news story about a young mother who had let a crying baby drop from her lap to the floor. The baby had hit her head and died. She was a few months old, the same age as our daughter was, when the story made the papers. Later, it was revealed that the baby had been crying nonstop for five hours in the middle of the night. I was horrified to realize that I understood exactly how this awful tragedy could have happened. The realization was a lifechanging moment for me. I can still recall the mother's name. There but for the grace of God…

Since then, I have met countless mothers who relate to this experience and who are relieved to know that they are not alone and that they are not bad mothers because of it. The ability to recognize such depth of feeling, such helplessness and such frustration, and then to separate these feelings from what we actually do about them remains, to me at least, one of the main challenges of parenting. Instinct is perhaps not about what makes a parent so vulnerable to extreme feelings. It is more about what stops us *acting* on those feelings. Perhaps this is the essence of the small amount of instinct that some of us are lucky enough to have.

Instinct can be extraordinarily useful if whatever you do turns out well, and if society approves of the outcome. It is pretty instinctive to throw oneself at a child who is about to run out into a busy street. It is also pretty instinctive to throw oneself at a child who is about to hit his baby sister again. The former may well be more socially acceptable. It is frequently instinctive to hit back, to seek revenge, to harbor negative feelings, to get even. There are times when we either may choose or are forced to abandon instinct and use our reason, our wit and our words to solve problems.

Till Death Do Us Part

As parents, most of us know that we love our children, or at least we're pretty sure we do. How we know that is sometimes a little hard to explain. Most of us know that, given the *Titanic* scenario, we would have sacrificed our own place in the lifeboat to our son or daughter—or at least we like to believe that we would. Many of us who watched or read *Sophie's Choice*, in which a mother is compelled to choose between her son and her daughter and ends up losing both of them, identified totally with the agony of her situation and silently prayed that we would never be forced to make such a decision. Most of us have experienced the warm, almost religious feeling that comes frequently over us, once our children are in bed and asleep. Awe, pride, wonder, gratitude, appreciation; this must be love. However, even on the days when things are going really badly—we're tired, they're tired, they're whining, we're whining—we don't usually plan on giving them up, well not that seriously—or at least only temporarily. When faced with any threats, real or imagined, to our children's well-being, we rise up and defend. We may show we love our children by what we say and what we do, or we may assume that they know it. It's often a little hard to know you're loved when you're yelled at all day, or when parents are never satisfied with what you are doing, or when they don't have any time for you because there is always something else that's more important, or when you're hit, or when you're lonely and sad and there's no one to talk to—or even when you're simply taken for granted.

There is little question that to "love" a child is to make a commitment for life. Our children need to know this and to keep on knowing it. Parenting is for life. They are stuck with us and we are stuck with them, however difficult life may become. You cannot and do not divorce your children. Most of us are fortunate also to experience the subjective feelings that go along with loving a child. Some children are easy to love. Some of us feel love for our children even if they are not very lovable! We try hard to make the distinction between loving and liking, and further, between liking a child but maybe not liking what he or she is doing. A child can certainly tolerate being told that someone does not like how he is behaving much better than he can tolerate being told he is not liked; but can any child tolerate being told he is not loved? Some children put up with the most appalling treatment from a parent in the vain hope that there is some love to be had somewhere in the relationship. Some children whose parents believe that true love is expressed through rigid and punitive discipline spend their lives believing that hate and love are usually indistinguishable—almost universally because this is how they themselves were raised. Some children whose parents equate love with permissiveness spend their existence begging for their parents to set them limits, so that they know that they are safe and that their lives are truly valued.

What children seem to need is the message that parents will be there for them—through thick and thin, for better or for worse, in sickness and in health, through the good times and the bad, including adolescence—and that they will have their parents' support, even if not their approval, right on into adulthood. The one thing that we cannot control, of course, is how we feel. If the feelings of love are there, terrific. If they are not, let's get on with the job as best we can.

When Love Is Lost

Ben and Marianne had three boys even though Marianne had not really wanted to have any children. She had felt pressured, not only by Ben who was from a large family and had wanted his own children ever since he could remember, but also by her friends and her family who gave her the impression that there must be something wrong with her if she didn't want to give birth. She and Ben had talked about her feelings on the subject since way before they were married, and both of them had been convinced that she would eventually change her mind. She didn't. In truth, she was quite happy being just a couple, enjoying her freedom and her job, and had never felt the stirrings of maternity within her breast or anywhere else.

At a convenient point in her career, when she was in her early 30s and when she was afraid that Ben might look elsewhere for a mother for his offspring, Marianne finally capitulated and took time out to have the children. Ben had wanted half a dozen. They compromised at three. Two, actually, but he didn't get his girl, so they gave it one more shot. By this time, they were a comfortably off, middle-class family with no money worries. Marianne could do some contract work at home, so she decided to stay home with the boys for a few years. Later, she speculated that she did so just to see if spending more time with them made it easier to like being with them. In short, she found that she not only did not like being a mother, she didn't even like the boys that much. Sure, they were interesting children. She had been quite content doing lots of things with them: taking them places like museums and libraries, as well as to parks and swimming pools; reading to them from the old classics and poring over nonfiction books and atlases; introducing them to educational and creative pursuits that she really enjoyed with them. But she never really bought in to the whole "mother" thing. She did not like babies and was frustrated when they could not tell her what was wrong so that she could fix it and stop them crying. She hated the world of play groups and nursery schools and used-toy sales. She didn't like the mess they made and had a hard time tolerating any whining or crying. She didn't know what to do when they were sick, so she got cranky too. By the time the youngest was two, she was back at work full-time and loving it. The boys were either in school or in day-care, and the individuals who looked after them when she was not around seemed to her to be doing a much better job than she could have done. They were patient and kind, listened to the trivial complaints and bickering, kissed the bo-bos, mopped up the messes and genuinely seemed to like the boys.

Marianne didn't particularly like any of her sons much. The oldest reminded her of her brother who had caused her mother all kinds of trouble and who had ended up cutting himself off from the family. He had an "attitude." The middle one was a "wimp" who whined a lot and was never satisfied with anything. The youngest was a "clingy" child who would not be left anywhere without a fuss when he was younger, and who insisted on sticking so close to her when she was home that she would trip over him if she forgot he was there. She had found that their arrival and the constant demands on her time had interrupted her relationship with Ben, and that it was difficult, if not impossible, to recreate what they had had. She resented the boys for that. Ben had become busier and busier and, although he spent time with the boys on the weekends, had delegated the vast majority of the child rearing to her. They tried to work as a team and managed to agree on all the big issues, but the implementation was left to her. Despite the changes in their relationship, the shift in priorities and the struggle to find time together, the relationship was solid and they were in it for ever.

She spent a lot of energy worrying about how she felt—or didn't feel—about her sons. But as hard as she tried, she could not generate the warmth or the "love" she thought she should be generating. It was not that she never felt it. It would probably have been easier if she had not; then perhaps she would never have missed it. It came in little bursts, here and there—so she knew what she wanted to feel. But she simply didn't feel it the majority of the time. She talked about feeling a bit detached from them, as if they belonged to someone else. She wasn't constantly angry or irritated with them or taking out her frustrations on them. She simply didn't feel much at all.

When Marianne was asked if she wanted out of the "mother" thing, she was quite horrified. She had no intention of leaving, either the relationship with Ben or the children. She had read widely and had taken some psychology courses, and so was concerned about the effects her feelings would have on the children, in terms of their self-esteem or their ability to form other relationships or in their lives in general. She decided that her goal was to make the best of the situation and to try to minimize any harm she might do to the children by her own perceived lack of warmth and love. She started to explore the job she wanted to do as a parent as being separate from how she felt about the children. She did this by looking from the boys' perspectives of what they needed from their parents—in a "minimal acceptable standard" sort of way. She sorted out what Ben provided and what she provided, and became a little more comfortable with the idea that, as long as the children had access to warmth when they needed it, it did not matter precisely which parent was the source. She wrote herself a job description that she felt she could follow and one which she felt would fit with what the boys needed from her. She began to deal with her middle son's whining and her youngest son's clinging without feeling guilty. She planned time for the boys so that she was not always feeling compelled to respond to their every whim; and she stuck with it, even if she did not always feel like doing so. As she made some changes, the boys' behaviors started to change and they became far less demanding. As a result, she did not find it quite as difficult to spend time with them, and they seemed to enjoy spending time with her. They found her interesting and stimulating—"not the kind of mom who just makes cookies all the time," one of them confided. Besides, she was the only kind of mother they had.

What happened was that Marianne began to give herself permission to "love" her children in her own way without living up to someone else's ideal standard. She realized she was in it for the long haul, so could stop looking at every hitch as a sign of impending doom. She began to explore different ways of being a mom that suited her better, and she found that she could actually say "sorry" if things did not work out as she had intended, or if she over-reacted—no groveling, just a healthy apology. She could see that her boys, although far from perfect, were mentally and physically healthy, that they were well bonded with her and their father, and that they were quite capable of making and maintaining friendships of their own. With her help, they were developing appropriate skills to become independent and were taking more than adequate steps to get there.

—•—

The Bottom Line

So what is the bottom line about this myth of maternal instinct? If you have it, how wonderful. Listen to it and make sure that it is accompanied by a good dose of reality checking and common sense. Don't assume that it is exclusively a female phenomenon. Some women don't have it; some men do. If you don't have it, remember that guilt is a self-imposed emotion. Don't worry, you'll manage. Go with the reality checking and common sense, and that will be a good start. Recognize that your children need mothering, and remember that mothering is not a gender issue. There is no shame in recognizing either that it is hard work or that you don't know how. Realize that there is no one else out there who can do the job for you, and set about acquiring the skills you need, whether this learning be from books, from other people, from courses, whatever. Show that you love your children by being committed to seeing them through to adulthood. Try to like them whenever you can.

Chapter 5

How Do I Love Thee?

Whatever Love Means...

Actually, the quote was: "Whatever *in* love means...," tossed out in response to the inane question as to whether Prince Charles and Lady Diana Spencer, upon announcing their engagement, were "in love." It got the Prince into all kinds of hot water later, once the public realized that it was probably an ominous portent of the disasters to come. In my view, however, he was spot on. What love means is an impossible question to answer, even when referring to the heated passions of romance and physical attraction, and the belief that we want to be with this one person for ever. What many couples, or at least one of the partners, discover is that the commitment till death is a wee bit too long and increasingly impossible to envision—and the number of divorces has been increasing at an alarming rate.

The explanation that "Mommy and Daddy used to love each other, but we don't any more and so we have decided to live in separate houses so we won't fight all the time" is frequently used to explain to children that the divorce has nothing to do with them, that it is an adult issue with the attendant adult responsibilities. What children *hear* is that loving relationships, ones that were promised to last until eternity, can come to an end. People can stop loving people, even if they promised to love each other for ever in church and in front of God, and then these same people can go away. Why, then, are we so amazed when children cling to the remaining parent for dear life and worry themselves silly that they can behave so awfully that this parent will also stop loving them and leave? Why are we surprised when they keep testing this limit? You said you loved me, but you said you loved

Daddy too. What did Daddy DO to make you stop loving him? What am I doing that will make you stop loving me? I know you're angry at Daddy. Now you're angry at me, so are you going to leave me? What do you mean it's different? How is it different?

Even children in intact families are not easy to persuade when it comes to defining love. Siblings frequently fight about who loves whom more, and in many cases the implications of "if you loved me you would..." creates opportunities to get more, do more, have more than one would otherwise have managed. Explaining to older siblings that a new baby will not change the amount or quality of love already being received is a hard row to hoe. Especially when the reality bears out the child's worst fears. Here is my new brother who was touted to be such fun, such good company, and no chance of making any difference to how Mommy and Daddy feel about me. The reality is that my life has changed totally, and not one inch for the better. I have to wait for everything. I'm not allowed anywhere near him in case I hurt him or something, and he's just a bundle of noise, dirty diapers and a magnet for grown-ups. I hate him and I want him to go back to where he came from. Now.

The Double-Edged Sword

Another situation that can prove confusing for children is that, when we feel deeply for someone, we feel deeply whether the feelings are positive or negative. Children, just like adults, are often frightened by the depth of anger they feel for those closest to them—in many cases, their parents—since they are fearful of being abandoned and so put themselves in a terrible bind because of their dependence on these same individuals. They may alternate between loving and hating, depending on the way the wind is blowing, especially in the turbulent years of early adolescence, when they rely totally on the "love" of their parents to keep them hanging on in the family. Most adolescents choose their friends over their parents primarily (although not necessarily consciously) because, if they're not chosen, friends will evaporate. Parents will not. Parents will go on loving you. At least that's the way it is supposed to be. Parents are expected to stick to their values, including their commitment to their children, so that teens can explore other planets and know that they can always return to home base. They don't expect home base to have moved while they've been away.

An Overdose of Love

On the other hand, there are many times when being instinctively protective, while innate and a big part of the job of mothering, is perhaps not such a great idea in the long run. This is especially the case for that part of parenting that involves teaching children to adapt to people and situations outside the family, and developing the tools they need when they go out into the real world.

———•———

Suzie was a superwoman. She was both an at-home and a working mom, having secured some word-processing contracts that she could work on in her own time at home when the children were asleep. She had two children, Debra aged six and Tommy aged four. She had breast-fed both children until they were three years old, and made all the family's food from scratch, preparing only organically grown food and eliminating any additives or preservatives from their diet. Her husband Charles was a busy accountant, who was pretty much absent from the family for a few months around tax time, but who kept an active interest in what was going on at home. He had clearly delegated the lion's share of parenting decisions to Suzie

———•———

and she accepted this delegation with delight. He was Tommy's Sunday School teacher and took both children to their swimming lessons on Saturday mornings. Neither child had ever been left with a baby-sitter other than grandparents when absolutely necessary, and neither had ever been away from home overnight without one or other of their parents. Two mornings a week, Debra had been involved in a very small, community-based nursery school program run by Melanie, another superwoman, in her home where the philosophy had been peace and harmony, cooperative games and conflict resolution. At home, no aggressive play of any kind was tolerated; even children's raised voices resulted in a gentle intervention and some quiet time for each child. All the rules of all the games at home had been adjusted so that no one lost. Even in "Sorry!" you weren't allowed to knock someone else's piece off the little circle to send them back to the start; you had to share the little circle instead. All reading material was carefully screened to eliminate any whiff of unacceptability and there was no television or VCR in the house.

Both Suzie and Charles were firm believers in democracy in the family, and the children were given every opportunity to express opinions and to vote on family plans. In order to get consensus on important issues, the parents occasionally lobbied the children behind the scenes, but generally both children had been quite compliant and could quite easily be talked into agreeing with the expectations and plans of the family.

The problems began when Debra started school. Kindergarten was an unfamiliar and uncharted territory. In kindergarten, Debra discovered that not everyone took turns; some people snatched and didn't respond very well when she used her words and said "I don't like it when you do that." They didn't even listen. The teacher was not much like Mommy and she had a voice that was quite different from Melanie at nursery school. The rules of the games let some people win and some people lose. Some people didn't even care about the rules; they just made them up as they went along. At recess, you didn't get to play on the climber if you just waited. You only got to play if you pushed. Jeremy pushed all the time and stuck out his tongue when you cried. The teacher was nice, but she let people talk loudly and even she talked loudly when she was angry. She got angry with Jeremy quite a bit. So Debra decided that she didn't want to go to school any more. She decided that she would much rather stay home with Mommy and Tommy and go back to nursery school with Melanie and play games where she didn't lose and people made sure she got a fair turn and nobody shouted or pushed.

Suzie and Charles tried everything. They coaxed and cajoled; they reasoned and debated; they tried to lobby for votes, but did not succeed. They decided that the problem was at school, because Debra was certainly very happy at home. So they went to talk to Debra's teacher. No matter how hard they tried—and they tried hard—the teacher would simply not agree to change the way she ran her program. Neighbors had said what a wonderful teacher she was. Well, Suzie and Charles did not agree. They tried to talk to her about how sensitive Debra was, and how she was used to being treated as an individual, not as one of a group. They even tried to pass on some of Melanie's ways of bringing out Debra's potential. They suggested that the teacher talk more quietly and that she try conflict-resolution strategies rather than direct instructions. The teacher listened politely and nodded in all the right places, but she still didn't change the way she ran her program. Efforts to take the matter to the school administration met with the same response.

Suzie decided to take Debra out of kindergarten and school her at home. Charles certainly was not wild about keeping her out of the mainstream, but Suzie said they would wait until they could be sure of getting a teacher who would provide the kind of nurturing environment Debra needed—and parenting decisions were Suzie's. They tried to persuade Debra to go back to school at the beginning of Grade I, but she had a male teacher who, said Suzie, did not relate well to sensitive little girls. So Grade I was not a safe enough place for Debra to be. She is now in the middle of Grade 2 and is still being schooled at home. Suzie and Charles have still not found a teacher who is willing to protect and nurture Debra as she is protected and nurtured at home. After all, Suzie says, school should be just like home, shouldn't it?

———•———

This is a somewhat extreme, but not that uncommon, example of how "love" in the guise of maternal protection can inhibit the development of skills that allow a child to handle the ups and downs of life in the jungle of school. For the most part, parents need to keep a vigilant eye on what is happening outside the home so that genuine issues of safety can be swiftly identified and dealt with. Incidents of aggression, intimidation or bullying frequently cannot be handled by the child alone; neither do they always have to result in an assault charge. In lower-key circumstances, the child sometimes needs back-up from behind to learn how to deal effectively with threatening or scary situations. He does not benefit from being put in the Catch 22 of being told to go for assistance when he feels he cannot handle it and then being accused of tattling and told to go handle it himself. Whenever there is a whiff of danger to either physical or mental well-being, adults need to step in. While we may see a vast difference between potentially dangerous situations and simple teasing or "play" fighting, some children do not. They perceive both as equally threatening. Therefore, they need our help to distinguish between various incidents, so that they can plan their responses effectively; and will judge as much, if not more, by our behavior as by what we say to them. Listening to the child's concerns with an active interest, allowing expressions of feelings, and then asking the child what action, if any, he would like us to take will frequently suffice. This is easier to say than to do when we are fighting the instinct to go flatten anyone who dares to threaten our baby.

You Can't Hurry Love

Doing the job of parenting is made far easier by loving our children, but we cannot mandate love. On the other hand, those of us who are lucky enough to love our children usually realize that love alone is not enough. We can still, in fact, raise mentally healthy children given an appropriate commitment and a willingness to do the job, even if we are not born warm and fuzzy. It is a wonderful gift to be able to love our children, to like them as human beings, and to feel that we are defined by part of them being part of us and that they are defining themselves by incorporating parts of us into their emerging characters. Building the unique mosaic that will be each of them is the job that we start and one that we supervise for a long time until they take over and complete the job themselves, but there are many other, sometimes unknown, influences along the way. Maybe the pattern turns out as we planned; maybe it turns out to be different. As insecure as we are, we tend to take all the blame and not much of the credit. The huge responsibility that accompanies the job of parenting frequently generates both an anxiety and a vulnerability that can dampen our unbridled enjoyment of our children, at least until we feel more comfortable in the shelter of experience.

Teaching children to express their positive feelings is important. Expressing our *own* feelings, using behaviors and phrases that model this for them, is one of the most powerful tools we have to hand. "I think you are really neat!" "Thanks, I appreciated that help," "Did I tell you lately that you're special?"—whatever we can muster, not forgetting the ubiquitous "I love you." Non-verbal expressions are not limited to hugs and kisses, bearing in mind that half the world are non-cuddlers! They also include random acts of kindness, smiles, silent company, handmade cards, little notes, and many idiosyncratic acts or gestures or pet names that are special because they have become special.

Whether we love our children or not, the job of parenting must be done. As Phillips Brooks has said: "Duty makes us do things well, but love makes us do them beautifully."

Chapter 6

Who Said Life Was Fair?

Born Equal?

As everyone who has more than one child knows, all our children are different from each other from the moment of conception. Even twins who share the same genetic makeup, cell-for-identical-cell, have different intrauterine experiences: one gets more space than the other, one's foot is in the other's ear, one is slightly larger, one is born first. So even *they* come out different.

Our own three offspring could not be more individual.

Our firstborn has always been intense, passionate, extraverted, adaptable, anxious, competitive, driven to succeed, and independent. She was lifting her head and arching her strong little back from the moment she was born and has been striving to get on with exploring and expanding her universe ever since. She had raging tantrums during her Terrible Twos that left both of us exhausted. My husband said that I was the only person he knew who could argue with a two-year-old and lose. But then things seemed to click and she learned how to fit into the system. Mind you, she never did things in the most conventional or predictable ways. She was far more interested in climbing in and out of the boxes that the gifts came in than she was in playing with the various toys the intended way. She quickly tired of stacking cups and rings and started to find unique uses for them. She hung upside down on the swing set from the top bar once she had discovered that this was more exciting than sitting on the little plastic seat. In fact, plastic seats were never her thing. Nor were strollers. Partly because of her need to explore her world actively, she has been the high achiever—also, no doubt, because her every achievement was always greeted with wonder and awe and lots of positive reinforcement. She was the first, so each step was also our first, and still is. She has never been content with anything less than the best, for herself and for others. She is at her most comfortable when she knows exactly what is expected of her and when she can give it. She has always invented opportunities out of nowhere and has spent her life faced with what she sees as an infinite array of options. Sometimes this is exciting and eternally optimistic. Sometimes it is overwhelming and leaves her full of doubt. Yet she has always learned something from every choice. Despite all this, I used to feel that we were reining her in, rather than encouraging her to grow! I sometimes still feel that way. On the path she has chosen, she will save lives.

Our middle child, being of the same gender, has always had a bit of an act to follow. She has done so by being as different from her sister as is humanly possible! As an infant, she was quite content to wedge herself, thumb firmly in mouth, in the corner of her crib and sleep the whole night through. When awake, she would sit contentedly for hours in the same plastic seats and strollers so despised by her older sister, observing her world and making mental notes. She followed her sister with her eyes and eventually on her hands and knees and feet—and observed. She learned by watching. She still does. She was the cuddler whom I could rock to sleep. She bypassed the Terrible Twos completely and could be quieted by a raised eyebrow or a look. Then she hit four. I remember quite clearly her sitting down in the middle of a shopping mall when we were on holiday in Vancouver—and essentially not getting up for the next 12 years. She has always hidden her lights under bushels, waited to be discovered, and blossomed when people have taken the time to find her and bring her out. She had two memorable teachers in Grade 5 and a guidance counselor in high school who all took the time—and we are grateful to them for that. She has had a struggle learning to express her wants and needs in words, and still frequently does so quite indirectly, suffering quiet disappointment and sometimes even despair when she is misunderstood. She has helped teach the rest of the family to read nonverbal cues. She has been our conscience over the years, quietly challenging our values and our reasons for doing what we do, and subtly changing them. She has taught us that when you think you know all the answers, the questions change. She is as deep as the ocean, fiercely loyal, easily hurt, sometimes irrationally sentimental, quietly stubborn, always on a mission, and a passionate voice for those who have no voice of their own. On the path she has chosen, she will save souls.

Our youngest has been the product of our benign neglect. We sort of gave up after the first two! By the time he was born, we already knew that he was different yet again. Besides which, whatever had worked with our firstborn had to be reinvented with the second—and we had no energy left to start over. He had been brought home from the hospital in his little plastic seat and was quite content to stay there—in front of the TV, on top of the washing machine, beside the jacked-up car in the garage, in the canoe, on the bicycle. In fact, one of the only things that has changed over the years is that the little plastic seat is now the couch and he has a channel-changer permanently affixed to his right hand. Fortunately or unfortunately, he was born into a family with experience. We have parented him with a tolerance, or lack of tolerance, developed on the backs of his sisters. He is not the vanguard of our self-esteem as parents; he is the beneficiary of it. He has always been different from the girls. I am intolerant of weapons of all kinds, in fact violence in any form. Yet he was born, as are most boys, with a genetic predisposition to fashion guns out of any available medium—sticks, spaghetti, Barbie dolls—and to race around the house armed with the inside of a paper-towel roll, uttering a guttural, and extraordinarily realistic, imitation of a semi-automatic. Yet he has turned into a peace-loving, non-aggressive young man who does not seem to have an enemy in the world. His dad has mourned the loss of his companionship, sharing a love of the outdoors, cross-country skiing, canoeing, biking, as his son has grown up and away. At 18, the brink of manhood, he is laid-back and content with life, athletic but not particularly competitive, fun loving and full of humor, friendly but not overly sentimental, both responsible and irresponsible, delighted to discover that the harder he works, the better he succeeds, happy with himself and his friends, on the edge of the nest and ready to go. On the path he has chosen, he will save sanity.

How could we ever have contemplated treating these three individuals equally? They were born to different parents disguised in the same bodies. Like your children, each one has had, and still has, different wants and needs, and each one has uniquely molded our parenting to fit his or her particular personality. Treating them all exactly the same has never worked and never will. In fact, to treat them all the same would be totally unfair to their individual differences.

Life *can* be fair, provided we do not confuse fairness with equality.

Is Life a Contest?

One of the driving factors behind sibling rivalry—the main generator of the battle-cry "but it's not FAIR!"—is frequently that children perceive themselves as being in a contest, with the prize primarily being parental attention, either in real or symbolic form. For example, children will jostle for air time at the meal table, seats next to Mom or Dad on the couch or in the car, goodies at the store, in an interminable effort to see who "wins." In an attempt to demonstrate to children that there is, in fact, no contest, and that they are all loved equally, many parents spend time they don't actually have trying to ensure that there are no "favorites" and that no one can actually win.

———•———

Mike was a widower with two sons, Joey aged 12 and Matt aged eight. His wife had died quite suddenly from a brain tumor when the boys were just eight and four, and Mike had been the boys' primary caregiver from that moment on. He had benefited from the sometimes overwhelming help of kindly neighbors and relatives for the first year or so, and had eventually settled into the life of a single parent, attending parent-teacher interviews, chauffeuring to extracurricular activities, concocting cookies for bake sales, staying home when the boys were sick, rushing them to emergency for an array of bumps, bruises and bacteria. He worked for a large company that was always threatening to downsize. So far he had kept his job, but, as he frequently said, "you never know…" The boys talked openly about their mom and the family had developed a pattern of small rituals to mark her birthday, the anniversary of her death and Mother's Day. Both boys were very close to their dad and there was much evidence of love and laughter in the home, despite all they had lost.

———•———

Mike sought help for Joey because his teachers were concerned that he might be quite depressed. He had pretty much shut down at school, was not completing his work in class and was quite sullen and withdrawn when they tried to reach out to him. His teachers were aware that his mother had died and had gone out of their way to be kind to Joey, but their patience was wearing thin and he did not seem to appreciate their efforts. At home, he was also somewhat on strike. He refused to do homework and chores, balked at the rules and was difficult about going to bed at night. He was occasionally quite physically aggressive with his brother, especially when Matt would go into his room or want to watch TV with him. Mike was at a loss as to how to handle this, and Joey was a somewhat reluctant participant in the quest for assistance.

It quickly became clear that, to Joey, life was totally unfair. Although his belief in this concept quite definitely had its roots in his mother's death, it was his father's treatment of his brother that, on the surface at least, was his prime complaint. Whenever they fought, Joey saw himself as being blamed and punished, even though he maintained that he never started it. He felt that he had far too much responsibility for Matt now that he was baby-sitting him after school, complaining that Matt would never do what he was supposed to do, and that he was again blamed for this. He felt that his dad's interference in his homework was unwarranted since he could manage by himself, and that it was unfair that he was expected to do chores that his brother was not expected to do. His three wishes were "to have my Mom back, to have a billion dollars, and to be an only child." His latent anger with his dad was countered by almost total dependence—and he was in the classic bind of knowing that he was constantly on the verge of biting the hand that fed him.

Further inquiry disclosed that Mike had instituted equal treatment for the boys at home. This was partially for his own convenience, time- and cost-wise, but also in the belief that he should give each one what the other one had to show no favorites and to keep the balance between the two. They had the same bedtimes and the same allowances. When one had a sleepover, so did the other. Pizza portions were virtually weighed to see that they were even, and cans of pop were measured to ensure they each got exactly half, to the drop. They were both enrolled in ice hockey and soccer. One new bike resulted in two new bikes, and Christmas and birthday presents were carefully priced to ensure that neither boy was favored. On the other hand, not all was equal. Joey was required to baby-sit Matt and to make sure he did his homework. He was supposed to clean his room. He was not allowed in Matt's room because he took stuff and didn't return it, but he complained that Dad told him off for trying to keep Matt out of his room. In an effort to deal with the situation, he was taking the law into his own hands—and becoming very discouraged at the consequences of his lack of experience and strategies. Both boys were engaged in a continuous struggle to see who could win additional concessions or outdo the other. They were hooked on the contest.

Discussions with Mike around the equality issue confirmed that the boys were extremely different in temperament and needs, with Joey more the introvert who kept his feelings to himself, and Matt the outgoing ball of fire. Mike also produced the insight that it was actually Matt that he was afraid of! He realized that, if he were to allow Joey some different privileges because of his seniority and his needs, he would have to face the wrath of his younger son, which was apparently quite something to behold. For his part, Joey—like the vast majority of children—was not able to debate the issue that being treated the same as his younger brother was somehow not equitable, at least not beyond the ubiquitous "But it's not FAIR!" Rather, he had begun to press the issue by accelerating his negative behavior.

If he hadn't convinced himself that it would save him time and effort in the long run, Mike might never have tackled the issue at all. However, he decided to experiment to see if a different approach would effect any change in Joey without bringing the ceiling down on all of them.

Once he was clear about what he wanted to do, he called the boys together and told them that they were going to try an experiment because he would like to see some changes at home. It wasn't a family meeting as much as an information session. Mike started by instituting a "zero tolerance for violence" policy. There was to be absolutely no discussion if either boy resorted to physical aggression; there was no reason that either could give him to justify a physically violent solution. The issue that had caused the aggression would be dealt with in other ways, but the aggression would not be tolerated. Period. He said that he was fed up with the constant bickering and that he expected them to make some suggestions on how to resolve the issue of the TV and the sanctity of their rooms. He told them to get back to him with these suggestions a week later, or else he would institute his own solution—which was no TV and both rooms off limits to the other. He also said that, because Joey was older, his bedtime would henceforth be one hour later than Matt's. "But that's not FAIR!" said Matt. "I know," said Mike. He also said that each boy's allowance would be tied to their weekly needs and based on individual discussions with each of them independently. Joey's allowance would include an extra amount per week to allow him to buy lunch in the cafeteria on Fridays and to take over the responsibility for buying his own junk food which Mike would no longer buy for him. "But that's not FAIR!" said Matt. "I know," said Mike. And he told them that, after school when Joey was baby-sitting, Matt would be in charge of himself in terms of his after-school "job"—that is, to stay in the house or the yard, to watch his TV shows, to get himself a snack and to write down anything that was a problem or that needed to be discussed when Dad got home. Joey, for his part, was also in charge of himself—that is, to stay in the house or the yard, to make sure that both he and Matt were safe, to get himself a snack and to start on his homework. It was also his job to report to his father with regard to issues that were safety related, morally threatening or unhealthy, and that were likely to get another individual out of trouble and not simply IN trouble. He was also to do this in written form, except, of course, in emergencies when he knew he could telephone his dad or otherwise secure help from the lady next door or other neighbors.

Unknown to the boys, Mike spoke to Joey's and Matt's teachers to tell them that he was trying to institute some changes at home and could they please let him know if they noticed anything different at school. He also requested that Joey's teacher tighten up a little on requests for work to be completed and gave her permission to deal with Joey quite firmly when such requests were ignored or not completed. He explained that Joey needed to know what was expected of him so that he had a way of winning back people's approval.

After a month of this experiment, there were some interesting outcomes to report. Joey's behavior had changed quite noticeably, both at home and at school. He was more outgoing and confident, and his sense of humor had returned with his friends. He had quite willingly been going to his room, actually in advance of his bedtime, to listen to music and read, and had not hassled Mike about it. He complained about Mrs. Kirby's personality transplant—he figured it was menopause— but he knuckled down and started to pay lip service to his assignments. He was tickled pink at his new-found "wealth," although for the first couple of weeks he had

had no money left by Friday to buy his cafeteria lunch. Despite his efforts at cajoling, Dad had not given him an advance, and by the third week, he had decided to put aside the lunch money in a secret place in his room so that it would be there on Friday. On the other hand, Matt's behavior had been quite difficult for Mike to deal with, as he had anticipated. The anticipation and predictability had allowed Mike to plan how to handle it, but it still came as a bit of a surprise. When it came down to it, however, Matt's complaints were primarily noise and bluster, and Mike was able to watch the picture and realize that, despite all the hot air, Matt was actually doing what Mike wanted him to do. The boys had come up with a time-sharing plan for the TV that was quite rigid but that seemed to be working, and they had decided to put large notices on their bedroom doors which ominously threatened dire consequences to those venturing to enter without permission. Initially, there had been quite a litany of written complaints from both boys when Mike came home from work; but because they were on paper, he had time to look them through after supper when he was feeling more human, and also to think about what he wanted to do about them, if anything. Mike had discussed with Matt some of the benefits of being the younger child—and was making sure that Matt received them, including some alone-time with Dad after supper while Joey was doing his homework. He had also ensured that Joey was receiving some benefits from being the older one, with his alone-time with Dad after Matt was in bed. At last count, Joey was reporting much lower levels of depression. Mike was considering taking Joey out of hockey next winter and putting him in skiing where he yearned to be, because he could take the ski bus by himself once he turned 13. Besides, Mike liked to ski. While Matt was still not certain that life was entirely fair, he could at least watch his TV shows without interruption and, if his door was closed, both Joey AND Dad had to knock and get his permission before they could come in. This felt good.

———•———

Fighting Fair in Families

As parents and adults in general, we tend to fan the flames of conflict in our efforts to make life fair, by trying to act as judge and jury when the only witnesses are the suspects themselves. We also provide a very compelling audience to prolong the performance. We talk too much and we try to fix everything. Contrary to the principles of the justice system, we judge based on prior convictions, often in the absence of evidence. As such, we set ourselves up as great people for each child to have on his side. Thus we perpetuate the contest for our attention and our support.

It is not possible to deal with all the complexities of sibling rivalry in a small section of a small chapter of a small book, and there are already excellent books on the market on this topic (e.g., *Siblings Without Rivalry* by Adele Faber and Elaine Mazlish, and *Kids Are Worth It!* by Barbara Coloroso).

Copyright © 1998 by Baby Blues Partnership. Reprinted by special permission of King Features Syndicate.

There are, however, several rules of thumb with respect to fighting in families that can help provide an approach until you have a chance to read these wise volumes. The Peace Education Foundation in Miami produces a wide range of programs designed to help children learn to fight fair, both at school and at home. The basic rules they lay down are:

- Identify the problem.
- Focus on the problem.
- Attack the problem, not the person.
- Listen with an open mind.
- Treat a person's feelings with respect.
- Take responsibility for your actions.

The reason that these sound like common-sense suggestions is because they are. Like most common-sense solutions, they disappear in the waves of emotion that usually accompany conflicts in relationships of any kind. So it is important to recognize the following:

Be realistic

Even in the best of families, there is conflict. Life is competitive out there in the real world, and it is necessary to prepare our children for this reality. Families that try to eliminate all conflict and bury all anger tend to produce children who are fearful and anxious in many normal situations involving other adults or their peers. Birthday parties, sleep-overs, trips to the park, school can all become looming disasters if you have no skills to deal with other children and the conflicts they engender. Always remember that there are limits to the times we can or should change the environment so that our children remain constantly comfortable. We have to teach them skills to cope with an environment that we cannot change for them. In this way, they are empowered to make changes themselves, rather than always expecting that changes come about only when others effect them.

Separate feelings from behavior

Feeling angry and acting angry are two different issues. We frequently confuse the two, albeit unintentionally. For example, we often say to children, "Why on earth are you mad at her for that? You did the same thing yesterday!" or "She's only little. She didn't mean to hurt you, so don't get so upset!" We need to allow children to own their own feelings, even if we do not agree with them.

Deal with the behavior

If the behavior is causing an immediate problem, it obviously has to be dealt with immediately. Time out to allow for cooling off is frequently helpful for both adults and children, even before feelings are expressed or acknowledged.

None of us does our best problem-solving in the midst of a crisis or a tantrum or when we are extremely emotional.

When dealing with the behavior, it helps if you can:

- describe what you see or hear (e.g., "There are a lot of raised voices in there." "There seems to be an argument over whose turn it is." "The window is broken.");
- tell how you feel (e.g., "I don't like it when that happens." "I get irritated when I hear that tone of voice." "I am disappointed that your promise wasn't kept.");
- state what you want (e.g., "I should like each of you to go to your room to cool down." "I want you both to play somewhere else." "Please give it back to her." "Please think over what you have done and let me know what you think I should do about it.");
- follow up.

Listen to and acknowledge the feelings

You may be able to do this first—or at least before you decide what the consequences, if any, are to be imposed for whatever the behavior was. This is one of the hardest skills for parents to learn and to carry through. We are often much too keen to judge and to fix. However, it is worth the effort, since it is frequently the missing piece in parent-child communication. Again, Faber and Mazlish have produced two excellent books on listening skills that are listed in the bibliography. In a nutshell, however:
- listen actively, asking questions if you must (e.g., "Tell me a bit more about..." "I'm not sure what happened after..."); this simply ensures that you get as much information as possible; try not to make it the third degree. Remember it is for clarification only;
- reflect or paraphrase what you hear (e.g., "So what you are saying is..." "It sounds as if..." "So Mr. James got very angry with you when you came in from recess."); do not judge what you hear. Simply restate it; this

buys time and allows both you and your child to double check that you have heard what is being said;

- label and acknowledge the feeling, even if you don't agree with it (e.g. "That must feel..." "I guess you were pretty upset about..." "I bet that made you nervous..."); many children cannot respond to "how did you feel?"; don't be afraid to risk guessing at how they feel. They will usually correct you if you are wrong;

- over the longer haul, help children expand their "feeling words" vocabulary to include words other than angry, mad, sad and happy; introduce them to such feelings as: frustrated, nervous, worried, anxious, irritated, disappointed, discouraged, excited, embarrassed, content, peaceful, proud, and any others you can think of—preferably by using them yourself!

No fouls!

Fair fighting means sticking to a set of rules and not permitting fouls. This is very easy to say in the calm of the day, but in the heat of the argument, fouls abound. The Peace Education Foundation includes such fouls as the following:

- ***Bringing up the past*** This means throwing in comments about actions, behaviors, events that took place in the recent or dim distant past. There are times when it seems particularly relevant to me to introduce issues that date back to the early years of our marriage when we get into a marital argument at home. As an extravert, I do this because they pop into my head. My husband is predictably sick of hearing them, because I dredge up the same things over and over again and shake them even after they're dead. "The pit-bull approach" is what he calls it. A therapist might argue that this is because the original issue has never been resolved. That therapist would be absolutely spot-on right. My husband will seldom admit he's wrong, which, in my mind, is frequently the only acceptable resolution. Introverts, however, are particularly good at dragging up old issues, primarily because they have only talked about them in their own heads and have not shared their concerns with the real world. The difference here between introverts and extraverts is that the individual listening to the extravert has heard it all before many times over. The individual listening to the introvert is suddenly incredulous at what has just come out. "What? But I didn't even know that *bothered* you!" is the most frequent response, followed closely by "What? What are you *talking* about?" The bottom line is that, to fight fair, one has to stick to the topic at hand. The phrase "That's not the issue. What we are talking about is…" can be useful here.

- **Blaming** This is an easy one to fall into, and we all do it, however conscious we are that it does not help and, in fact, makes matters worse. Any statement that begins with "You…" especially if it implies a wagging finger, and especially if it includes the word "always" or "never," is suspect in this regard, although this foul is somewhat insidious and can crop up in very subtle ways. Put-downs are included here, and are not to be tolerated.

- **Name-calling** While it can and does occur independently, this particular foul is closely associated with blaming, in that it tends to occur when one is attacking an individual rather than a behavior. It can crop up even in the most benign circumstances, slipping out in the midst of genuine attempts to resolve conflict positively. "When you…, I feel… because…" can, for example, degenerate into "When you yell at me, I feel hurt and humiliated, because you are such a crude, loudmouthed jerk." "I don't like it when you refuse to eat what I cooked for supper. I would prefer it if you weren't such a selfish pig." Many families disagree on what constitutes name-calling. This is usually based on each individual's own upbringing and the slang of the day, and it is impossible to set a given standard of acceptability across families. Therefore, it is important for each individual family to establish firm guidelines that may be quite different from one family to the next, given individual needs and sensitivities. While the term "loser" may be marginally acceptable to some, it may be totally inappropriate to others. It is important to make the guidelines perfectly clear in any family where name-calling is a particular problem and may need to become a zero-tolerance situation (discussed later in Chapter 10) especially where children have special needs and certain words are pejorative.

• *Physical aggression and/or intimidation* A total no-no. Period.

Be mindful of the fact that some degree of conflict is normal, natural and necessary—even if it is nauseating—even in the most loving of homes. Totally avoiding conflict or eliminating it completely are unreasonable goals, since the world outside the family is certainly not conflict-free and our children need appropriate strategies to deal with it. Learning to deal with conflict, particularly others' anger and disappointment, is a life-long task for many of us. Now remind me again, *who* said life was fair?

Chapter 7

Teamwork

The "Management Team"

Raising children who will live in the 21st century requires teamwork. Even if we are single parents, it is virtually impossible to raise children alone in our complex world. In addition to taking advantage of access to extended family members, friends and neighbors when we can, we delegate much of our parenting responsibility to the institutions that our society has created to support us — child-care facilities, nursery schools, schools, hospitals, dentists, piano teachers, Scout and Guide leaders, pubescent camp counselors and swim instructors, school-bus drivers, teenage baby-sitters and countless others. These form the modern equivalent of the global "village" that it takes to raise our children so that they will acquire survival skills.

Regardless of the number of individuals and institutions involved, however, the primary "management team" consists of the parents — together or apart, loving or hostile towards each other, cooperative or competitive, competent or incompetent. We have a job to do, and we have about 18 years to do it. Our goal is to produce a rookie adult, functioning independently, complete with the roots of all the skills he will need to survive in the world outside the family. The requirement to work together on this particular task is something many of us take for granted, but many of our children grow up with parents who live apart — in different houses, different cities, different parts of the world. Fortunately for the children, in the majority of these cases, both parents are still involved, still trying to parent in partnership with someone whom at best they tolerate, at worst with someone whose name and face they cannot even bear to hear or see. Parenting is a difficult enough job when we like each other; it is sometimes next to impossible when we don't.

In the workplace, many of us are used to working with others on a given project. For the most part, we accept that the other members of the team have different personalities from our own, divergent views of the world, disparate philosophies of life, a range of talents quite unlike our own. Wherever we can, we must use our differences to maximize the group's range of competencies. We have a job to do.

Getting Our Act Together

The emotional load that accompanies the role of parent can both help and hinder us in this job. Our children clearly need the parenting team to pull together. When the emotional climate of the family is disturbed, the balance of the entire group is threatened. This is sometimes very easy to see, but extraordinarily difficult to correct—and our children's behavior may soon reflect the general unrest in this climate of discontent.

——•——

Rachel was a seven-year-old only child whose parents had separated when she was just turning five. They had negotiated a rather tentative joint-custody agreement so that they would each have equal access to Rachel. On paper, this was so that she would spend an equivalent amount of time with each of them. In reality, it was because neither of them could bear the thought that the other partner would "win," Thus, promptly at 5:00 p.m. on Sundays, Rachel picked up her suitcase and waited at the end of the driveway for her other parent to come to collect her. Her parents communicated via heated phone calls and the occasional bitter, face-to-face exchange, which sometimes resulted in Rachel crying and hiding in her room.

It was Rachel's dad who decided to seek some help for her. He felt that she was desperately unhappy. She was complaining of tummy aches almost every morning and headaches almost every night. Yet multiple visits to the doctor had not uncovered any potential physical causes for her symptoms. She had missed several days of school over the previous few weeks, whimpering in the mornings when it was time to get up, and escalating into inconsolable sobbing when the school bus arrived. Her dad left at the same time that Rachel left and he was arriving at work increasingly late and exhausted. He had tried asking his ex-wife whether there were any problems at her house, but her responses were always evasive at best and scathing at worst. It was no good asking Rachel. The parents had agreed that they would tell her not to talk about what happened at the other house, because, they had explained, they did not want her to feel responsible for being a messenger. The Grade 1 teacher was expressing concerns, not only about Rachel's frequent absences, regardless of who the current custodial parent was, but also because she refused to join in any of the Grade 1 classroom activities, crying for no apparent reason, rejecting the advances of her friends and shutting down as far as work was concerned. It was clearly not going to be possible to work directly with Rachel, at least not initially. On the one occasion her dad managed to get her to the office, she refused eye contact, clung desperately to her dad's arm and stuck to his side as they sat on the sofa. She would not play with any of the toys or take advantage of the offer of paper and markers. Interestingly, she was not in the least bothered at the suggestion that she might wait in the next room; in fact, she could not leave the office fast enough. The paper, markers and some of the toys accompanied her. Her dad was then able to speak freely about his worries. When the session was over, Rachel asked if she could take home the picture she had drawn spontaneously. It depicted Dad's house on the one side and Mom's house on the reverse side.

Separate sessions with Rachel's mother and father enabled each of them to vent about the other and eventually to get down to working on what they wanted for Rachel. Despite their open hostility and animosity towards each other, they were surprisingly similar in both their short-term and longer-term goals for their daughter. Both were open to looking at what Rachel needed to make some sense of a life that was totally different from the one she had enjoyed only two years previously. Both were concerned about what was happening at school and at home—even though each laid the blame soundly at the feet of the other—and both wanted to help Rachel return to being the happy little girl they both remembered. With very little encouragement, they each managed to put together a "job description" for her. First, they listed their expectations for her in a general way. Next, they expanded this to include more specific behaviors. For example, they both wanted her to be in school—going to school was not negotiable for either of her parents—and they expected her to make some effort in the classroom. They wanted her to have time to play with her friends and to pursue extracurricular activities. Dad was keen to have her help out around the house because he believed that this helped children feel they were active contributors to the family. Mom felt that Rachel was pressured by this expectation to help out and so had chosen the route of expecting very little. She said that children deserved down time after school. However, she was not happy with the amount of cleaning up she found herself doing after Rachel had swept through the house. Therefore, she was willing to consider having Rachel do some daily and weekly chores. They both agreed that a set bedtime was good for all of them. This would give Rachel the reassurance of a regular routine and the grown-ups some adult time in the evenings. They both worked on a set of "non-negotiables" for Rachel, including going to school, wearing her seatbelt in the car, speaking politely when she wanted to be heard, and remaining on home property when she was playing outside at either house. They also agreed on providing her with nutritious food, expecting the little homework she brought home to be done, and on guidelines for when she would be considered to be sick enough to stay home from school. They each agreed to finance half the cost of her ballet lessons and to take her to the ballet lessons regularly, whichever house she was inhabiting at that point.

So that she would not become too overwhelmed, they agreed to pick one area of concern and to work on that first—and, surprise surprise, they both chose the morning routine. Thus, Rachel's job was to get up, get dressed, eat breakfast and brush her teeth. After that, she was permitted to choose some activities for her "down time" until the school bus came. At Mom's house, she chose to watch cartoons. Since morning TV was not a choice at Dad's, she picked playing in the back yard with the dog when the weather was nice and rummaging through Dad's big box of comic books when it was raining or snowing outside.

Without ever meeting face-to-face to discuss any of this, Rachel's parents managed to agree on a communication book to be passed from one parent to the other at the weekly hand-over point. This book would not be given to Rachel; however, she was to be made aware of its existence so that she would believe that necessary messages about her health, various appointments, school events, dates with friends, ballet recitals, etc., were being communicated between her mom and her dad, and so that she could make sure that important information, that she wanted shared, could be shared, without the need for World War III. Both parents sat down with Rachel individually to explain to her what was going on and how they were working together to make sure that life ran more smoothly for her. Her homeroom teacher agreed to meet Rachel as the school bus arrived, until the mornings settled down. The principal offered to involve the school mental-health worker to do some low-key counseling with Rachel at school to help her to express her feelings through art and play, even though there was a long waiting list for the service.

Almost immediately after her parents instituted the plan, Rachel began to settle down. There were very few tummy aches or headaches, and those that did appear did not in any way prevent her from going to school or carrying on with her normal life. She responded well to her "job description" and kept track of her progress in a little book of her own, awarding herself endless stars, happy faces and other symbols of her pride in her small successes. Her homeroom teacher reported that, apart from the occasional glum face on a Monday morning, she was once again joining in classroom activities and her mind seemed to be back on her work. By the time she was at the top of the waiting list for the mental-health worker, she no longer needed the involvement. After several weeks of decreasing anxiety, her parents actually managed to speak to each other on the telephone to make arrangements for the summer holidays. They did not agree, of course.

---•---

Vive La Difference!

Most of us choosing a lifetime partner do not sit in the back of the Chevy or in the darkened basement discussing what our various child-rearing approaches will be. Nor do we tend to select a life partner from the ranks of those who have similar personalities to ourselves. But we spend our children's childhoods striving for consistency. This is something like driving a tank through a minefield, blindfolded. While it is incredibly important for a child to know what his parents and teachers expect of him, and equally vital that promises of consequences are kept wherever possible, being consistent, in terms of how we achieve our goals, is far more elusive. By the time they are preschoolers, our children can tell which one of us will give them a precise decision and which one will allow them to procrastinate and buy time—often to the point where the original issues are long forgotten. They will quite readily adjust to these two different styles—far more so than we adults do. Many parenting couples spend hours trying to persuade their partners that everything would be fine if only the other one would have a personality transplant.

Copyright © 1998 by Baby Blues Partnership. Reprinted by special permission of King Features Syndicate.

When a team is formed to work on a particular project, in almost any situation other than in a family, it is almost certainly a given that the various team members will bring along different sets of skills, training, background, experience or personality characteristics. It is also quite likely that the differences will be valued, rather than resented or criticized, since the project will clearly benefit from the widest possible range of tools and ideas. In fact, the broader the range, the better the project can be.

Parents, on the other hand, frequently spend inordinate amounts of impotent energy trying to change the other partner—especially trying to change his or her mind about a particular approach, a specific incident, a viewpoint or behavior. The reason we persevere for so long is that it sometimes works and we know from behavior theory that intermittent reinforcement is the most powerful reward schedule. Thus, the occasional brick giving way will keep us banging into the wall for much longer than we would ever have anticipated, given our overall level of success, which is usually miniscule. In other words, except for some rounding of sharp edges and mutual mellowing with the years, we tend to retain the approach to life that we brought into the parenting relationship. Those of us who love to process information and to make decisions will continue to do so. Those of us who never believe that we have sufficient information to make a decision will continue to find ourselves in a dilemma. Those of us who are extraverted will continue to share our every thought as soon as it enters our consciousness to get the feedback we need to evaluate our every thought and feeling. This means that others will share in our constant decision-making or our eternal dilemmas, whether they wish to or not. Those of us who think that others cannot be remotely interested in our thought processes will carry on our internal dialogue, sharing only once we have made our decision—that is, if we are also the kind of person who ever makes a decision; otherwise we agonize internally and no one knows the trouble we see.

Parenting requires a lot of extraverted attributes: the ability to act on little or no information; the ability to adapt to change at a moment's notice; and the social niceties associated with such perennial parenting jobs as attending parent-teacher interviews, making small talk with other parents at various sporting events and running the Brownie bake sale. On the other hand, parenting also requires some important introverted characteristics, such as introspection and planning, the ability to understand another's need for space and privacy, and the loyalty required to stick it out through the rough times.

Parenting also generally demands instant decision-making—the seat-of-the-pants type that children need at the same moment that we are on a critical long-distance telephone call, the second the dog has thrown up on the rug, or the instant that we have to be out of the door to a meeting. We have to make decisions about what to make for meals, what to send to school for show-and-tell, what to tell our children about strange Uncle Joe. If we are natural-born organizers, these decisions will not faze us much, although we may change them often and eventually run out of ideas. If we are not intrinsically interested in or do not feel competent with making even minor decisions, but prefer a more flexible approach to life, we may well be the better listeners. Much of the time, our children are not asking us to organize their lives; they are simply asking us to hear what they are saying.

In any parenting couple, two of us who have the same characteristic may get on well superficially, but sooner or later the world will demand something different, and one of us has to adapt. We will probably not be happy adapting, and we may well feel stressed. In fact, we may revert to our original personality preferences as soon as possible. The introverted parent from an introverted parenting team who ends up being the social convener for the family will probably get burned out sooner or later, and will resent the other partner for not doing his or her share. The child of the extraverted, organizing parenting team will feel bulldozed and will beg at least one parent to take the time to think before they fix everything.

As partners, it is always helpful to try to be aware of and to understand our differences. When our differences complement each other, we can be awesome. When they collide, we can be awful. Learning to appreciate each other's differences, and to recognize that *different* is not necessarily wrong, despite what our own upbringing tells us, are the primary tasks of couplehood. These tasks may need to be tackled before we can provide the united, team approach that will most benefit our children.

Good Cop, Bad Cop

We have all seen TV police and detective shows where one of the partners works the criminal over with the hard-nosed, aggressive approach, getting nowhere. Subsequently, the other half of the team arrives on the scene, whereupon even the most hardened offender appears to be willing to give up the whole shot in exchange for a cigarette and a kind word. Parenting is not too different. Sometimes the scene is pretty much exactly as above, with the possible exception of the cigarette. Or it can be the reverse situation, with parent A spending hours being nice, persuading, cajoling, coaxing and even bribing, all to no avail, while parent B shows up, barks a single-word command and the child's opposition miraculously melts. Having parents balance each other like this can frequently work very well. Children can be quite overwhelmed by two parent Bs or can be endlessly controlling with two parent As. However, it takes a lot of cooperation and understanding to perfect the team approach, so that each parent plays each role some of the time. The main danger is that one parent gets stuck in the "heavy" role, while the other is the perennial "rescuer." This can cause irreparable damage, not only to the partnership but also to the relationship between each individual parent and the child. In an extreme situation, such relationships may perpetuate an abusive situation or may create a totally passive child who develops no problem-solving strategies of her own, but instead expects to be saved or bribed. A break in proceedings for a quick and private "management" meeting can frequently clarify goals and jobs. Children are thrown slightly off guard when parents retreat for a discussion and come back with a united front, and this can serve to break an otherwise unpleasant impasse. It is important for us to give ourselves permission to retreat from the battle front to discuss strategy, and it is unwise to hold such strategy sessions in front of our children, since they will be quite happy to pick whichever side is the easier one for them and to lobby actively for that particular position.

Working with Caregivers and Teachers

If it isn't bad enough trying to get it all together within the parenting partnership, we are then faced with the issue of working together with all those individuals to whom we delegate a vitally important part of child rearing—our children's education. Whether this begins with a local baby-sitter or day-care provider, or whether it starts only at the beginning of compulsory schooling, the issues are essentially the same. If our children are to benefit from our combined energies, these energies need to be working toward the same end—that is, to the benefit, not the detriment, of our children.

There is no question that, before children enter the formal school system, we, as parents, not only have some freedom of choice in determining which other adults we permit to assist us in our function of raising and education our children, we actually have an obligation to ensure that these individuals are worthy of that responsibility. Although there may be many practical constraints, we can pick one baby-sitter over another; we can switch whenever necessary, and we can pretty much guarantee that our children will not be left in the hands of someone we consider to be, at best a wrong "fit" or, at worst, potentially harmful to our children's safety, mental health and general well-being.

Few situations are more harrowing than discovering that, once our children have entered the large, formal, public education system, we have little or no control over selecting the individuals who will have a far-reaching influence on our children's minds—the homeroom teacher, the music teacher, the physical education teacher, the whatever teacher. There is nothing like the feeling of hopelessness that comes with the knowledge that our child is stuck with a teacher who appears to have no understanding, no compassion and certainly no credibility, when it comes to standing *in loco parentis* for our child each day of the school year. In many cases, asking for the child to be transferred to a different class is either impossible or thwarted by an administration that either does not see the situation the same way, or is reluctant to take on the unpleasant process of attempting to discipline or remove a staff member. In many cases, parents are reacting unreasonably to normal limits and constraints placed on children, when they enter a system that is NOT a family and that is required to follow certain philosophies with which the parents may simply not agree. Many parents would like teachers to keep their children happy and entertained at all times, challenged to reach their potential, whatever that potential might be, and persuaded rather than required to carry out the various tasks inherent in a day's worth of school. However, many parents, especially those of exceptional students with special needs, have serious issues to discuss, and it is essential for all parties that a forum for communication be provided.

Fortunately, the vast majority of our experiences will be positive—even when our precious bundle is just a number among 140 new entrants to kindergarten, or an anonymous face in a class of 500 students in Introductory Biology at university. There are times, however, when we are faced with having to deal with someone whom we perceive as being less than kind, less than competent and perhaps, even less than human! While it is always an option to follow a formal route through the school administration—and this route should be followed if there is any reasonable suspicion of bizarre or abusive behavior on the part of a teacher—it is frequently more constructive to try to set aside the emotion from the situation, to try to define the problem as it presently exists for the child, and to combine forces to resolve the conflict.

Don't Forget the Children

I should note that it is my personal belief that children have no place in any initial discussion among the significant adults in their lives—especially when there is conflict among the adults—be they teachers, parents or both. In fact, the only time that I believe children have a place in parent-teacher interviews is when only positive information is to be disseminated. The trend toward pupil-led, parent-teacher encounters is fine and dandy. It has its place, but that is NOT to replace a genuine need for communication among the adults around issues of concern so that a plan of action can be put into place.

This does not mean, however, that the child should be left out of the loop completely. In many situations, the child is blissfully unaware that he has a problem, while his parents and teachers are at their wits' end to figure what to do. Over the years, I have seen a large number of children and adolescents whose parents cannot speak about "The Problem" with the child present because the child has no idea that the parents are concerned. For example, during my wonderfully educational stint as a school psychologist, I was called to one particular school to deal with a little boy in Grade 3. The classroom teacher had been concerned about him for a while because he was exhibiting some behaviors she felt were associated with high anxiety. Both the principal and teacher were quite agitated on this specific day because he had started to suck on the sleeve of his sweater. Both reported that he was reluctant to make eye contact, barely spoke when adults spoke to him in the hallways, and that he only had one or two friends in the class. To cut an unecessarily long story short, the "anxiety" problem was basically solved when this youngster was asked: to please stop sucking his sweater; to make sure that he looked at people when he spoke to them; and to make sure to acknowledge greetings from teachers with an appropriate response. While life is by no means always this simple, we have to make sure that we don't miss the obvious.

As Freud may or may not have said: "A banana is sometimes just a banana."

A child needs to be told what is expected of him in school and at home, and needs to be able to please the various adults in his life by complying with these expectations. Thus, before the child is introduced to the situation, the adults must define the issues, put them in positive terms that the child can understand and follow, and determine what options, if any, the child has to choose from. At this point, the child's opinion can be sought and any alternative, constructive suggestions the child has can be incorporated into the plan. This approach gives the child a real sense of involvement and of being listened to in a safe environment, in which he knows that the adults are prepared to support him and to work with him toward an effective solution.

Practical Suggestions for Effective Parent-Teacher Conferences

The following guidelines are adapted from a wonderful little book called *Counseling Parents of Exceptional Children* by Jack C. Stewart that came free one time with the hundreds of dollars' worth of books I have ordered from book clubs over the years. As the title indicates, the suggestions were originally intended for teachers. With some changes and adaptations, I have found them to be equally useful for parents—and, as a matter of fact, in many potential conflict situations in life. The general thrust is towards cooperation, rather than conflict, and the main purpose is to ensure that the best interests of the children are kept to the fore.

Treat each individual with respect
This is a common-sense start to any interaction, but it is so often missing. It involves remembering that each parent and teacher is an individual, with his or her own concerns about the child, the school, teachers, parents and the world. Many teachers are parents. At any given moment, the way each of us

sees an issue represents our reality to us at that point in time. We act on our perceptions of reality. Our perceptions of reality may be different to each of us and each of us may be right. However, whether we are considered to be right or wrong, each of us is entitled to our own opinion.

Decide in advance what needs to be accomplished

This will help keep the meeting focused on the goals and will be more likely to keep the discussions relevant. For example, we may want to ensure that our child is receiving some help in an area of difficulty, or we may want to give some information, or we may want to express an opinion. It is frequently useful to jot down the main points ahead of time. A close friend of mine routinely dissolved in tears when she went to parent-teacher interviews. Her list was always written in a form to be thrust into the teacher's hands if she couldn't manage to say what she wanted to say. Sometimes it is worth establishing an agenda at the beginning. At other times this is not possible or necessary. But if we have an idea of what we want to say—especially if we are introverted and tend to defer to the extraverts in the group—it is worth taking a moment to run through our lists, preferably aloud, at some point during the meeting.

Ask permission if we wish to take notes

This is really just a courtesy, since we are each entitled to take notes if we wish. However, it is very important to extend this courtesy. Many of us do not have the memory of an elephant and simply need to jot down information as it is presented. It is important to be aware that even note-taking can be perceived as aggressive and adversarial. As a psychologist, I expect my clients to have access to my notes. Therefore I write them with that in the front of my mind. This is not out of place in any note-taking situation, especially in our litigious society. If we intend to take notes, regardless of the other person's consent, it is probably better to state this in a gentle form ("I am going to try to jot some of this down to help my memory later."), rather than to ask ("Would you mind if I take down a few notes so that I can remember it later?"). While most adults would anticipate that the other party would not mind, we are then stuck in a situation when she does. It is not particularly professional or realistic to expect to tape-record a meeting. It is much better to summarize the key points as you go along and then jot them down afterwards, or to ask the other party to summarize their issues in writing, if they are important enough to warrant it.

Begin and end with a positive and encouraging comment

This is known as the "positive sandwich" and is based on what are known as the "primacy" and "recency" effects in psychological memory research. We remember what we hear first and what we hear last—at least as far as determining the general climate of a discussion is concerned. It also reminds us that it is necessary to say something positive to prevent the baby from being thrown out with the bath water. There are certainly teachers out there, especially in some junior high school and high-school settings, who are fully entrenched in the idea that the only purpose of a parent-teacher interview is to point out a child's faults and deficiencies. There are also some parents who find it extraordinarily difficult to say anything positive about their children. Thus, we can set an example for each other by starting the meeting with a positive statement, even if it is vague or not directly to the point; for example, to a teacher: "I heard that you did a wonderful job with the choir at the festival." "Your classroom is so bright and cheerful." Something more to the point is more effective; for example, to a parent: "Philip is such a considerate little boy." "Melissa is so full of life!" or "Jimmy always tries his best." There is a fine line between being positive and being sucky. Watch it! There is quite an art to wording some negative statements positively. "Jeremy needs a little help to curb his enthusiasm." "Darlene can be reasonably successful getting along with the others when she puts her heart into it." We have all read between the same lines, whether we create or receive children's report cards. If a meeting has gone poorly and/or the conflict has escalated, it is more difficult to finish on a positive note. However, it is very important to try. "I really appreciate the time you have taken out of your busy day" is great; "Thank you for your time" will do, if nothing else springs to mind or lips. We all have to be careful not to be so nice and positive that the main point of the meeting is missed. I have met parents whose children are in terrible straits at school but who come out of meetings having completely bypassed the main issue: that their child is in dire need of help. I have met children for whom a repeat of grade is recommended even though their report cards are glowing commendations of their achievements and personalities. Be direct, but be constructive. Many parents report that a teacher contacts them to deliver negative information only, and many teachers report that they do not have the time to make calls to parents unless there is a problem. It is rare for me to hear that a parent has contacted a teacher to make a positive comment. It is my belief that we all totally underestimate the power of a positive word.

Don't rush the meeting

Be sure to set aside enough time to cover all the issues. Both parents *and* teachers can be guilty of trying to handle important issues in five minutes. However, beating around the bush is sometimes easier than getting to the point, so it is important to make sure that you don't take it too easy. Those of us who have attended multiple meetings in all types of settings realize the value of having someone keep an eye on the time. If the discussion is incomplete, the meeting can be reconvened. It is important to recognize the difference between venting time and planning time. In a situation where a particular child is causing trouble to many teachers in school and feelings are running high, it is important for those teachers and/or parents to meet and to vent *before* setting up any kind of constructive planning meeting with parents, since venting has a tendency to expand to fill the space it is given. Having an independent individual "chair" the meeting can be helpful.

Listen actively

Active listening involves attending to other people, following what they are saying, and ensuring understanding by checking out what we have heard. This is all regardless of whether or not we agree with them. It is very hard to listen actively when the other person is hostile, negative or putting forward a viewpoint that has no basis in our concept of reality. However, it is crucial, since we ourselves have no credibility unless we do. "So what you are saying is…," "If I understand you correctly, you believe…," "According to what you are saying, Jonathan…," "So your three main points are…," are all examples of active listening. It enables us to paraphrase what the other person is saying without editorializing or passing any kind of judgment. It merely ensures that we have heard correctly. Given that ninety percent of communication is non-verbal, we must be aware of whether our words and our body language are saying the same thing. We must be especially careful to control our facial expressions of disapproval, contempt or anger, and to watch for sarcasm in our tone of voice.

Be willing to agree whenever possible

Agreeing with the opposing party is a well known strategy for disarming an opponent in any argument. It is none the less so in parent-teacher or parent-parent conflict. It is incredibly difficult to do, but works so well that even an initial successful stab can be very reinforcing. "You are quite right, he can be very difficult" sets the stage for cooperation, whereas "What are you talking about? He's only difficult because other people are being unreasonable!" escalates the conflict. Even if we add a huge "but," the initial agreement does not usually go unnoticed: "I know that she can sound extremely rude, but…" at least validates the other person's concern to some degree, although it sets the stage for a potential rescue which may not be helpful to the child. It is far preferable to agree wherever we can and leave it at that. When it is patently obvious that we do not and cannot agree, remaining calm and stating our opinion without hostility opens up the possibility for communication. "I hear what you are saying about Meredith's behavior. However, I believe that…" suggests the active listening scenario described above and breeds constructive discussion. Agreeing to disagree is a mature stance that can be taken in some circumstances with some individuals. The bottom line is that the child cannot be left in limbo while the two most important sets of adults in her life reach a passive impasse. Action may still need to be taken, even if the parties cannot agree on who is to blame or who has won. It is not a contest.

Explain so that others can understand

True communication takes place only when both the sender and the receiver have the same information. We each have an obligation to express ourselves as clearly and precisely as possible. We also have the right to ensure that we have understood what the other person is saying. We all have a tendency to assume that, just because we have said something, the other person should have understood. Too frequently, this is a misconception. I have met a number of individuals who did not realize that they had cancer after a physician had told them that they were suffering from, for example, carcinoma or Hodgkin's Disease. I have met even more who were told that their children had "visual-spatial deficits" or "problems with non-verbal analysis and synthesis" or "dyslexia." There are still surprising numbers of individuals who feel intimidated by jargon and by "professionals" who use it, and who, therefore, feel embarrassed or self-conscious or just plain stupid if they ask a question. Picking up and using the other person's own vocabulary and phrases can be useful as a means of ensuring proper communication, and the use of specific examples or related analogies can also be quite enlightening. "As you say, he has some run-ins with his buddies in the neighbourhood whenever things don't quite go his way. It's a little like that with me in the classroom." "You say that he is quite inappropriate in his way of interrupting in class. I guess you mean that he's a bit mouthy?" Once again, it is important to emphasize acquiring the ability to paraphrase what the other person has said to ensure mutual understanding. Bear in mind that some other people know more than we do and some other people know less—and it is frequently impossible to know who is who!

Agree on at least one action step each

Rather than trying to resolve a whole issue in one shot, it is frequently helpful for each party to agree on one small action that will be in the general direction of an overall solution. Specific information and action can often minimize the hopeless-helpless feeling for both parents and teachers in situations where a child is having a particularly difficult time. In any situation involving both parents and teachers, it is assumed that the child *alone* does not have either the answer or the power to make the necessary changes. Therefore, it is unacceptable for a meeting such as this to end with neither set of adults being able to think of a single constructive thing to do. However small, each party needs to agree to something. Parents, for example, may agree to contact their family physician so that the child's general health can be checked out, while a teacher may agree to initiate a particular expectation in the classroom or in the school yard. It must be kept in mind that neither agreeing to go for family counseling nor having a principal shadow a teacher for a week constitutes a "small action." Engaging the child in the loop at this point is also usually appropriate—for example, agreeing on an expectation for a child that will be communicated to him by both parents and teachers and that will be monitored by both. The importance of a positive job description cannot be over emphasized, and will be dealt with again later.

Summarize, plan and follow up

At the end of the meeting, it helps to summarize quickly what each person has understood, especially in terms of who has agreed to do what and what happens next for the child. If the chair of the meeting does not do this, it is acceptable and worthwhile for either a parent or a teacher to initiate it. I often suggest to parents or teachers that they follow up a meeting, especially a complex or difficult one, with a short, pleasant note outlining what they understand was agreed upon, and what they themselves have contracted to do. The same rules about starting and ending with a positive comment apply. If the note is written in the heated aftermath of an emotional encounter, my advice is to sleep on it for a day or two, and then rewrite it without the need for emotional catharsis or the inclusion of any provocative statements. Remember that a letter will form part of a documentation process should there be any difficulty. It also provides a means for other parties to respond and to put on record any corrections or alternative perceptions they may have of what occurred or what was planned. Finally, ensuring that we follow up with our part of the deal is critical—not only does it show an investment in both the child and the resolution of the issue, it also shows our children appropriate behavior and establishes a climate of trust within which both children and adults will benefit and blossom.

Chapter 8

Visions and Values

Mission Statement

A number of years ago, all the members of the department in which I was working were transported out of the office into a pleasant country hotel for a two-day staff retreat. Having three youngsters at home at the time, with little or no opportunity to travel on the job, this was more a treat than a retreat for me. It gave me an opportunity to get to know those individuals with whom I had been working better. We spent much of the time hammering out a "mission statement" which was supposed to encapsulate the overall philosophy of the department in a few simple lines to provide us all with a *raison d'etre* and a direction that would guide our future decision-making. The rest of the time, we socialized. Whether it was the result of the partying or of the more serious seminars and discussions or all of the above, we managed to come up with both a mission statement that reflected our commitment to support the children, families and schools we served, and that really did seem to blend our various goals, whether we were psychological service providers, social workers, speech-language pathologists, administrators, teachers of children with special needs, whatever. For the life of me, I can't remember what that mission statement was. All I recollect is that we came away full of energy for our "new" direction and for a while working life looked beautiful once again.

Many of you will also have experienced something similar at work, a "bonding" experience that serves to re-energize and to cohere the group, along with some degree of validation for one's sense of belonging and sense of purpose. But how many of us have ever done something like this within the family? Maybe you have been lucky and your religious group or community group has provided a family renewal experience, but most of us know nothing of such opportunities. Yet it is very difficult to make sense out of all the various decisions we make daily as parents, unless we have an overall purpose and general direction.

To have a "vision" as a family means putting some thought into the type of family environment we should like to have in our home: a climate of mutual respect, a healthy lifestyle, a stimulating atmosphere for the communication of ideas, a creative milieu for encouraging artistic or musical growth, a spiritual direction, a group of individuals with positive self-esteem who are able to love and to be loved. The possibilities are endless, and sound remarkably as if violins should be playing in the background as we speak. Many of us have enough trouble simply keeping our heads above water and frequently feel worn out trying to make ends meet. Even those of us who would like to subscribe to a vision are often discouraged once we let ourselves think about how on earth we would go about doing this! Usually, this discouragement leads us to give up before we even start, especially if we are constantly at odds with our partner, whether that person is present in the home or not, trying to deal with the daily battles and weekly wars that are fought on home turf.

When the members of a parenting couple do sit down to talk about their visions for the family, it is remarkable how similar those visions are, particularly for parents who have made a sincere and deep commitment to each other and to their children. Perhaps it is the similarity of vision that enables them to commit to the long-term. Perhaps it is the long-term commitment that enables them to have a vision. Who knows? Who cares? The important factor is that mission statements can be formulated for a family. They can reflect the general philosophies of the parents and shape the daily expectations for each other and for the children. These mission statements can be broad or narrow, general or specific. They can relate to a specific family goal in the present, or to a comprehensive 20-year plan. Each individual can have his or her own mission statement, or there can be one vision for the whole group. They are shaped by our values and by what we feel to be important in life in general.

It is very hard to find words for other families' mission statements; they are frequently too individualistic. An example of a broad, general, altruistic vision might be something like: "We are committed to enhancing the self-esteem of each member of the family by encouraging, enabling and supporting each other to achieve our individual goals." In fact, in real life, a family might have a vision like: "We are determined to get through the next few years without losing our sanity or our shirt and preferably without abusing our children or each other." Some more specific mission statements might not be quite so basic. One single mother had a vision that went something like: "My main priority for the foreseeable future is to find myself as a woman and to ensure that I get my own back on all the men in the world." A widowed father dreamed of beating all odds and winning the Boston Marathon. This necessitated another vision of having to develop an endless network of baby-sitters to mind the children while he trained. An example of a more specific mission statement that focuses on present-day issues would be along the lines of: "In our family, we are concentrating on making enough money to pay the bills" or "We pledge to regain some control over the children's behavior" or "We are committed to getting the house ready to sell" or "We are investing all our energy into preventing our children from breaking up our marriage" or (like Yvonne in Chapter 2) "I am devoting all my time and effort to doing everything for my children so that I can be a Good Mother." The possibilities are endless, and we all have a number of them, spoken or unspoken. If I were into giving you homework to do, I would suggest that you sit down and try to figure out your mission statement(s) at this time.

Family Policies and Decision Making

As I said earlier, the main purpose of having a mission statement or a vision is to facilitate day-to-day decision making. It is not so difficult to decide whether you are going to eat another serving of chocolate pudding if your mission statement has something to do with healthy living or if it has to do with pampering and indulging yourself. The outcome will be different, but the choice will be less agonizing in the presence of a directional statement of purpose.

Using the analogy of the family being rather like a small business in which Total Quality Management is practiced (see *Who's In Charge? A Guide to Family Management* by yours truly for a broad look at this approach), policies are the value systems at work in the home. When our children are small, it is the parents' values that rule. As they become young adults, they begin to develop their own value systems, or policies, to govern their lives. They may or may not be the same as ours or even based on ours, although the latter is likely to be so if we have provided a warm and nurturing environment for the value systems to be sown and tended. While value systems tend to differ slightly from family to family, a core of values seems to be shared by most of our friends, relatives, associates and acquaintances in the micro-culture that we develop around us. We tend to choose to associate with families with similar notions about safety for our children, about appropriate social behavior, about educational values, about mutual respect. We may choose not to associate with those who do not share similar values—even if they are among our closest relatives or even if they turn out to be the person we chose for a partner. Coming to terms with similar and different values is something that long-term couples manage. Producing a common set of expectations, or "procedures," for children is one of the outcomes of that management.

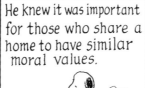

He began to feel uncomfortable with others in the family.

He knew it was important for those who share a home to have similar moral values.

So the dog left.

PEANUTS reprinted by permission of United Feature Syndicate, Inc.

Some examples of mission statements, visions, values and specific expectations are given here simply for illustration. There is no such thing as THE definitive set and these are not presented as a "thou-shalt-have-these-values" list. Unfortunately, or perhaps fortunately, no one can do that for us. This requires ongoing work, evaluation, fine tuning and more evaluation.

Vision 1

In Our Family, We Choose to Live in Mutual Respect

Sample Policy

Sample Procedures

In our family, we do unto others as we would have them do unto us.

1. When a bedroom door is closed, we remember to knock and wait for permission to enter.
2. When we get ourselves a snack, we remember to ask other people if they would like something.
3. When we wish to be heard, we speak in a voice that others can listen to.
4. When we wish to borrow something, we ask, and we return it in at least the same condition that it was in when we borrowed it.

In our family, we treat each other with respect and dignity.

1. We speak to each other in a reasonable way, using a normal voice.
2. We let each other know if there is something bothering us and we expect to help to work on a solution.
3. We respect each other's privacy on the telephone, with friends and in our rooms.
4. We inform parents to get someone *out* of trouble, not into trouble.

Vision 2

In Our Family, We Nurture a Sense of Responsibility

Sample Policy

Sample Procedures

In our family, education takes priority over leisure activities.

1. We do homework before we do chores.
2. We take family vacations only during school holidays, unless we have no choice.
3. When we have no choice but to take family vacations during school time, school work is brought along and is expected to be done.
4. We expect to pay for our children's education until the end of high school.

In our family, we do the "have to"s before the "want to"s.

1. We do our homework before we expect to watch TV or play with our friends.
2. We have our own share of community responsibility (like dishes, meal preparation, cleaning the house, etc.) and expect to do it.
3. We expect favors only after we have completed what we know we have to do.

In our family, we believe that children learn best by experiencing life for themselves.

1. We expect our children to earn their own way through post-secondary education.
2. We provide a basic allowance for our teenagers, but we do not give loans or advances.
3. We expect our children to find a part-time job during their high school years.
4. We do not rescue our children from the consequences of their own informed choices.

Vision 3 | In Our Family, Individuals Are Treated Fairly

Sample Policy

Sample Procedures

While we value each individual equally, we believe that we each have different wants and needs.

1. We each have a bedtime that is suitable to our age and that takes into account our need for sleep.
2. We do not get something just because everyone else does.
3. Each individual's wants and needs will be considered separately from each other individual's wants and needs.
4. In some cases, seniority is a sufficient reason.
5. There are sometimes different rules for adults than there are for children.

We respect freedom of speech.

1. We are each entitled to hold an opinion.
2. There is a time and a place for expressing an opinion.
3. Opinions expressed inappropriately will give rise to a consequence.
4. The "government" is not obliged to act on the opinions of the people.

The Messages We Send

As you read the previous few sections, you probably realized that, like most of us, you have never actually put much time into verbalizing your vision or your policies. We tend not to. I don't know about you, but during the court-ing stage of our relationship, my husband-to-be and I did not sit down and talk about what our policy direction would be with respect to homework or teen birth control or even financial responsibilities. This has meant that, over the years, we have had to make a great many arbitrary decisions, often rely-ing on impulse, plain common sense, seat-of-our-pants judgment…and damage control. Fortunately, each of us lives by a basic value that tends to result in decisions that have some consistency, both within ourselves and with each other. However, even given some consistent foundation, whether by chance or by design, there have been many times that we have realized belatedly that one or other of our children has picked up a message from us that we definitely did not intend to send!

Both children and adults are notorious at hearing what they want to hear. Each and every one of them will conclude what they wish to conclude, if we leave a tiny vestige of doubt in what we say. "But you didn't say I couldn't…" is a basic example of this, as in: "In our family, we each take care of our own things" spawning the misunderstanding that "I don't have to take care of anyone else's."

The main problems with misperceptions of policy frequently occur despite every good intention on the part of parents. The result is that essen-tially positively oriented plans to instill healthy self-esteem backfire.

Good Intentions: In our family, we believe in…
- keeping our children as happy and as comfort-able as possible
- giving our children reasons for what we expect of them
- using conflict-resolution and mediation to reach consensus
- providing a stimulating environment

There are few among those of us who like to be thought of as reasonable, "Nineties" parents who would not have goals like this in our parenting repertoire. In fact, all these aspirations have been found to enhance child development and self-esteem. Therefore, they are the basis of many a positive-parenting approach. While we probably should incorporate such values into our child-rearing practices, we must be alert for the possible backlash.

Messages Received:
- I expect to be happy and comfortable at all times
- I will do things if you give me a good reason for doing them
- I expect to be part of all the decisions made in the family
- I expect to agree with all the decisions made in the family
- I do not expect to be bored

It does not take too long to find out that these messages can have unfortunate consequences—or can at least push many parents' guilt buttons when we find ourselves apparently caught in a contradiction. We believe that our children should be happy, but we are frequently instrumental in causing them unhappiness, especially when we have not lived up to our own stated values! We do not always have a good reason for what we expect. Some parental decisions are made unilaterally without consultation, and there are many situations in which children are highly unlikely to agree with the adult position.

Even if they have never discovered it before, by the time they go to school, children learn that not all adults are as perennially benign as their parents, and that the rest of the world does not hold them in such high esteem. They get the message from the Real World that life is tough, that it's a jungle out there, that it's first come, first served, that nice guys finish last—and, most painful of all, that there's a pecking order in almost every situation for which they must, for the most part, compete. So, as parents, we must somehow reduce the stress brought on by this growing realization—to both ourselves and our children—that the way we would like things to be and the way they often are can be two completely different worlds.

Frequently, we have to add another message or two to the original list to make sure that our children are prepared to face reality.

In our family:
- we prepare ourselves to deal with disappointment and discomfort
- we learn from our mistakes
- we accept that we sometimes have to yield to authority
- we believe that out of boredom comes creativity
- we recognize that life is tough.

Testing the Waters

As our children are increasingly exposed to the world outside the family, they become more and more aware of the different value systems bombarding them from all directions—from the baby-sitter to their friends to their teachers to the media. During adolescence, in particular, it is a child's job to try out some of these different policies of life. This is the way they see which ones get which reaction from whom and which ones seem to fit in with what they want for themselves in their embryonic life beyond home. Before they are set to leave the nest and to make their way successfully in a world that remains, to some degree, unknown to us as parents, they need to have established a high degree of independence and a set of value systems that will guide their path.

———•———

Seventeen-year-old David had apparently managed to have pierced most body parts that were customarily on view to the public—and a few more. It was hard for me not to drool as he clattered his tongue stud against his teeth. His blue-tipped Mohawk hairdo was certainly eye-catching, and he added to the intimidating sight with his studded jacket, steel-toed boots, spiked dog collar and chains that dangled ominously from his belt. He was 6' 2" with broad shoulders and a permanent two days' growth of beard (how do they do that?). He had been in trouble with the police in the community a few times, almost exclusively for being in the wrong place at the wrong time. His parents were concerned, not only about his community escapades, but about the increasing number of calls they were receiving from the school regarding his "attitude" and his lack of appropriate deference to authority. He was fast approaching the end of Grade 12 with post-secondary choices looming on the horizon. His reputation, as reflected in his report cards, was one of "bright but must apply himself more," "would have a better mark if assignments were completed and handed in" and "organizational skills need improvement." As with most students, his marks reflected completed assignments that had been handed in. He was not doing well. During the last year or so of school, he had become increasingly withdrawn from adults and attached to his peers, many of whom were also individuals who were not academic bright lights and who tried to outdo each other in the let's-shock-the-adults category.

David's parents were both highly educated and successful professionals who were struggling with their parenting approach to their son. Their younger daughter in Grade 10 was not posing them any problems, but they had always agonized over David. Mom had worried that teachers did not appear to realize how bright he was and how frustrated he would get with his written work when he was unable to write as quickly as the thoughts that were tumbling around in his head. Dad tended to be more concerned with David's general attitude to his teachers and other adults, and was anxious to preserve the good reputation of the family in the small community they called home. Both had always believed in respecting their children and had used a fairly permissive style of parenting, trusting that both David and his sister possessed good judgment and common sense and that, with a warm environment at home and a nurturing style, the children would learn by example and pick up appropriate behaviors and values along the way. This approach had worked for many years but they had recently started to question whether they were doing the "right things" and had sought help to ensure that David did not go off the rails.

Discussion with David revealed that, appearances to the contrary, his value systems were pretty conservative. He had "been there, done that" with everything from booze and drugs to sex, and discussed them with a worldly wise attitude that belied his years. When he was pinned down to specifics, his own "policies" were roughly as follows:

I don't believe in drinking and driving.

I don't believe in drinking just to get drunk.

I don't do drugs any more.

I believe that people are who they are regardless of how they look or dress.

I don't smoke around my parents because they don't like it.

I do what I have to do to get by in school.

I always use a condom when I have sex.

I don't respect people who don't respect me.

I am entitled to my own opinions.

Beneath all the trappings of his times, he was a sincere, thoughtful young man. While his parents had not necessarily provided him with the precise list of policy statements as quoted, there was certainly evidence that many of their own values had rubbed off. "We believe in mutual respect, discovering and setting our own limits, accepting people for who they are, keeping ourselves safe." He was modifying them and adapting them for his own use and his own ends, which on occasion was getting him into some hot water. He was starting to be a little concerned that his marks were slipping. Therefore, he had to deal with the dilemma of compromising one or two of his beliefs to succeed over the next year or so of school. His opinion was that he should not have to do what stupid teachers told him to do just to get better marks, and he was definitely not going to give up any time with his friends to do more school work. His overall plan included spending some time backpacking through Europe or South America, coming back to college or university and getting a job that gave him the kind of lifestyle to which he was accustomed.

Discussions with his parents managed to edge towards a compromise over his behavior at school and in the community. Once they could see that his value systems were pretty solid, albeit not expressed in the terms they would have used, they were able to trust his decisions a little more readily. They had not yet allowed him to have a part-time job (it would take his mind off his studies) or a driver's licence (he was not showing enough responsibility), but would agree to look at a total package where David could perhaps earn his driving lessons by working for the money. They were also more comfortable agreeing to lift his weekday curfew (he was not, in fact, allowed out at all on "school" nights) provided he spent a couple of hours on homework—although all three of them recognized that he could not be forced to learn. David readily agreed to this and asked that his parents get off his case about his smoking and about how he dressed. Dad felt strongly that parents had an obligation to stay on a kid's case if he was putting himself in danger. David felt that he was fully aware of the dangers and did not need any more nagging. David was certainly in that blissful state of adolescence where he felt invincible and invulnerable to the threats to his safety that his parents saw all around him. Dad finally came up with the notion that he would write out all of his concerns about the smoking and that, should he have reasonable grounds to suspect that David had been indulging in this habit, he could have David read the entire list aloud to him and sign it.

The issue regarding respect was an interesting one to discuss. There was clearly a strong message within the family that mutual respect was both expected and valued. What had not been typically aired was the notion of whether respect had to be earned or whether it was a feeling, a behavior or both. David's parents took the view that a certain level of respectful behavior towards adults was certainly expected, whether or not that respect was actually sincerely felt, but they had difficulty with the idea that their children should automatically respect others, regardless of the other person's degree of respect for them. Like David, they felt that everyone was entitled to an opinion, but, unlike him, recognized that there was a time and a place for that opinion to be expressed. As in many families, there was no simple solution to this issue and David's parents continued to struggle with the ethical dilemmas that these views presented.

In the short term, David began to learn some ways of working within the system to his advantage: being more polite in order to change his reputation with one or two key teachers; spending a given amount of time on his homework so that something would be done and handed in; "contracting" with some teachers in classes where he had missed assignments so that he could catch up and hand the work in for reduced marks; liaising with his guidance counselor, whom he respected, to elicit support for dealing with potentially difficult situations. He did not change his friends or his way of dressing, nor did he remove any of his body ornaments—and he was proven right in his belief that many people continued to judge him more on how he looked than on who he was. However, he managed to get through high school with slightly better than mediocre marks and the last I heard he was working out West on an oil rig—Mohawk and body ornaments (except for tongue stud) cast aside for the moment in favor of more immediate issues: saving money for his backpacking trip and university.

Right and Wrong

Whether we like it or not, an intrinsic part of parenting is to teach our children about what is right and what is wrong. Those of us fortunate enough to have firm spiritual beliefs can take guidance from them in this area, since we believe in a higher power that distinguishes good from evil. Even with this background and support, it is not always easy to come to terms with what we actually believe, and, in these days of rights and freedoms, it is frequently difficult to equate one's own beliefs with political correctness. As a society, many of us have come to the conclusion that we should lay out both sides of an issue and let our children choose their own viewpoint. On the other hand, many of us worry that our own values will be lost in the process. As a result, we may try to block or color the opposing viewpoints in an effort to entrench our own.

As parents in the nineties, we are experiencing an information explosion that was unknown even ten years ago and we are almost powerless in controlling our children's information input. However much we try, by censoring what they watch, read, log on to, are exposed to in any way, we are tilting at windmills too numerous and large to conquer—and we may feel overwhelmed and give up, deciding that we cannot possibly compete, let alone win these battles.

We could not be more wrong. More than ever, children of the millennium need parents to know and uphold their own value systems. These represent the stepping stones in the quicksand, the oases in the desert. They are the secure basis from which to explore the moral environment, in the manner that toddlers explore their physical environment, needing to return to find parents exactly where they left them, not shifted, not changed, not absent.

Provided that we recognize that our children *will* explore alternative values—in fact, it is their job to do this during adolescence—and that this is normal, we can afford to stick with our own. We must teach them what we believe to be right and what we believe to be wrong and why we believe this. More importantly, when our children are young, we must act in accordance with our beliefs, if we are to have any credibility whatsoever or if we are to earn our children's respect. In other words, we must uphold our value systems by creating expectations that are in accordance with these systems and we must follow through to make sure that our policies are acted upon. A debate with an eight-year-old about his rights over his own body may well take place, but his own views may well not take precedence if he is deciding to put his own body in danger or to risk his health. As children get older, we must let them know that we respect their right to hold their own opinions and that their opinions may well differ from our own. As Voltaire is reported to have said: "I disapprove of what you say, but I will defend to the death your right to say it." However, understanding that there is a time and a place for expressing an opinion is part of learning to be mature, as is respecting the various authorities that govern our lives, even as full-grown, independent adults.

Visions and values are an intrinsic part of the parenting dynamic; some would even argue that they are the most important part. Without them, the everyday decisions become fragmented and often arbitrary, and both parents and children are deprived of the chance to understand that there is a bigger picture of humanity within which we can all learn to function and to be secure.

Chapter 9

Love and Limits

Positive Job Descriptions

Once upon a time, a long time ago, a not-so-young psychology doctoral student got herself a training placement in a setting where she was reporting to someone who did not understand the need for a positive job description, that is, being told what one IS supposed to do, what the expectations ARE. She was welcomed warmly, shown to her desk, introduced to colleagues, briefed on the general goals of the program and told to go ahead. She, being enthusiastic and not a shrinking violet, did not need to be told twice, so she did, albeit with some trepidation. Asking for further guidance did not appear to be expected and was met with a blanket "whatever you feel is appropriate." It was wonderful to be given this degree of trust and freedom. This heady dream pretty soon turned into the worst nightmare. The supervisor's "Do you have a minute?" became an invitation to disaster. "In this department, we do not..." became the general message that was given in small bits of information. "We do not call Social Services under those circumstances." "We do not put that sort of note in a file." "We do not send that documentation to parents." "We do not pick our noses in public." (Well, perhaps not quite, but you get the picture.) When she asked, she was told that no, there was not in fact a protocol in place for when Social Services should be called, nor a listing of what was to be placed on file or sent to parents. "Whatever you feel is appropriate," rather than an invitation to discovery learning and freedom, took on the flavor of a set-up.

This sent our fictional friend into paroxysms of anxiety. Finding out what is expected by tripping over what is not expected neither served to enhance learning nor to bolster self-esteem. In fact, it turned an enthusiastic, active and half-way competent individual into a dysfunctional, quivering mass of self-doubt who was afraid of her own shadow. Suffice it to say that the tale had a happy ending, thanks to the end of the placement, along with some kinder mentors and a good friend or two. However, the moral of this story is that success can be gained only when one knows how it is defined.

How "success" is defined will differ in specifics from person to person, but there are some universals in our expectations for those we love. If we love our children, we want them to be happy human beings. We want them to love and to be loved. We want them to find the positive side of life. We want them to be content with themselves and their choices. We want them to be able to form and maintain relationships with others. We want them to achieve their goals, whatever those goals may be. In short, we want them to find success in every area of their lives. As parents, we owe them the benefits of our greater knowledge and experience by setting up some signposts as to how to achieve this success.

In other words, to help our children to succeed in life and to reassure them that we love them, we must set them clear limits and achievable goals.

Yet many children live a life full of rules that are expressed in negative form; for example:

Don't hit your brother

Don't eat with your mouth open

If you don't do as you are told, you won't be able to…

Stop pushing

Stop doing that

with very little guidance as to what IS required, at least as a next step. To some degree, they then suffer the anxiety of our friend, especially in situations where there is no vision or value system to guide their decision making.

In addition, as the adults in the situation, we get stuck tracking negative behaviors and attending to them, and then having to find some negative consequence or punishment for the behavior we observe. We frequently run out of consequences in such circumstances. Whenever I am called into a situation where "we have no more consequences left," I know immediately that a negatively worded job description has been in effect. It is very hard to reward a child consistently for not doing something. "Wow, Candice, great not-spitting!" "Terrific, Michael, you haven't pulled anyone's hair all morning!" This is exactly like asking people not to think about pink elephants. The forbidden thought is the first thing that enters their heads and we are all focused on the precise behavior we have been trying to extinguish.

Some children are BORN knowing what to do to get a parent's or a teacher's approval, how to behave in any social situation, or simply how to succeed. These are the fortunate few. Most of our children, at some time or other during their development, need clearer guidelines on how to behave, sometimes even in what we would see as the most obvious of circumstances. For example, what their "job" is when we have visitors, or in Sunday school, or when a friend is over to play, or when they are at someone else's house. Many children learn what their job is at someone else's house and yet fail to learn that they have essentially the same job at home: behave like a human being and remember everything we have told you about manners. They have somehow received the message that this job description does not apply with parents or siblings.

Working out a child's job in a given situation is the key not only to security, but also to behavior change—in families, in school, at soccer, with friends, in life. For example, letting a young child know that he is expected to sit on the mat during circle time, to get on with his work when he is asked, to take turns with the other children and to listen carefully for instructions before he starts a task are all critical to his success in a school setting, as well as in life in general.

Wording this job description in terms of what is to be done gives a child the means to earn positive approval. We, the adults, are looking for what we want, rather than what we don't want. We will therefore reinforce positive behaviors, both advertently and inadvertently, simply by tracking them. Even very young children can learn what their job description is.

Before we go into specifics of a couple of techniques that can work, we need to understand the basic tenets of behavior underlying all that we do in attempting to "manage" our children and each other.

Behavior 101 for Parents and Teachers

The following are a baker's dozen of the basic rules of human behavior that apply in a wide variety of situations when raising children, whether or not we believe in behavior modification.

If it works, do it again

Simply put, if whatever we did resulted in the desired outcome, we can try repeating what we did. This has the strong implication that we have to be aware of what we did that worked—and this is not always easy when we are parenting. Sometimes it can refer to something we have deliberately set up, hoping for a given outcome, especially when that "something" is an informed choice with a predetermined consequence, as in: "When you choose to use a nice voice, I will listen to what you are trying to tell me."

If it doesn't work, make sure it is set up properly and try it again anyhow

This refers to something that we have tried to set up with a predetermined consequence that did not work out the way we had expected. For example, we had planned to give our child the choice of being listened to once he could speak in a nice voice, but we responded when he continued to whine, especially if we gave in to what he was whining about. We will have noticed that we are still mad at him and resentful of what we "had" to do. Our plan clearly did not work. This does not mean that we have to think of something new and different. We simply have to set up the choice and consequence clearly and actually follow through with what we had decided to do. If we dropped every technique and strategy simply because it did not work the first time, we would run out of ideas by lunch time. If we put thought into the plan before we try it and we stick to it, the chances are high that it will work. We must also be prepared for a child to "test" the plan by escalating his behavior at first. In other words, he may well get worse before he gets better. If a child immediately ups the ante or changes tactics, hang in—we are in fact being successful.

If it really doesn't work, try something different

I should like to have a dollar for each time I have heard "…but I've told him over and over again." If telling him over and over doesn't work, try telling him once and letting the consequences happen. Or try something non-verbal if words are not working. Acting predictably gives our children a great sense of security. Acting unpredictably sends them off guard. Sometimes, we can act unpredictably to make behavior change. It is a very powerful technique for a normally yelling parent to respond in a cool, quiet voice, just as it is for a calm, nurturing parent to shout. Children take notice.

A behavior that is reinforced will increase in frequency

This is one of those basic psychological definitions—a reinforcer is *anything* that results in a behavior increasing in frequency, including negative behaviors. Put another way, if a behavior is not going away or is increasing in intensity or frequency, it *must* be being reinforced. In some instances, it is a major challenge to figure out what we are doing that is causing a particular behavior to continue, in particular a behavior that produces negative responses in parents. It is hard to understand why screaming at our children or responding in some other negative way results in the repetition of the very behaviors that produced this response. It appears to be a fact of life that, for reasons unknown to all parents, children appear to prefer negative attention to no attention. Some mental-health professionals have been known to surmise that this is related to the ultimate fear in all of us—fear of abandonment—and that having a parent there yelling at you is always preferable to not having that parent there at all. There is also the issue that children do not always define "reinforcement" in the same way that we do. They do not always care about what we see as potentially reinforcing. However, never believe a child who says "I don't care." Watch the picture. Despite what the sound track is saying, if the behavior increases in frequency, we have reinforced it.

Depriving a behavior of its audience usually results in extinction of the behavior

Telling a child that the audience will be taken away does not work. The audience actually has to leave. This can be accomplished by using a time-out procedure for the child or by taking a good book, a cup of tea and a Walkman into the bathroom. In our house, there have been days when the dogs were given a number of extra walks. Occasionally, pulling up a chair and sitting in pregnant silence can also halt the show. In her comic strip *For Better or For Worse*, Lynn Johnston, the cartoonist-cum-psychologist portrays a wonderful scenario in which little April, aged two, is having a super tantrum in the laundry room behind her mother's back as she folds laundry. When April finally notices that Mom has finished folding and has left the room, she gets up, wanders around the house until she finds Mom again, lies down and continues her tantrum. How often have we been there? Unfortunately, we far too often provide an environment that particularly encourages our children to continue to perform. Then we are even angrier at the waste of the time we are somehow willingly giving. In any such situation, we can give our children a clear choice as to how to prevent the forced separation: if they choose to stop, they (or we) stay; if they choose to continue, they (or we) leave. These techniques and variations thereof are discussed at length by Barbara Coloroso in *Kids Are Worth It!* and by Thomas Phelan in *1-2-3 Magic,* among others.

A behavior that is learned can be unlearned

Thank the Lord. However, it is not easy to teach old dogs new tricks. It is far better to try to establish desirable behaviors when children are young so that they have the roots of whatever they need in adolescence or adulthood. However, it is never too late to try to effect some changes, even if the only change, as we have said before, is in our own behavior. One's theories about behavior can have a big impact here. If we believe that children are born with certain behaviors, or if they take after one of us or a relative, we may feel less instrumental in effecting changes, and we may feel somewhat helpless in the face of behavior we don't like. The belief that some children just have "bad blood" is particularly defeating and non-constructive. While we are all born with certain predispositions (for example, to be of a calm temperament or to have an irritable central nervous system that causes a high level of response to stimuli), the impact of our environment is phenomenal and is highly significant in shaping how our predispositions manifest themselves in our daily lives.

To establish a new behavior, it must be reinforced each time

This means that you simply cannot afford to ignore behaviors at first when you are trying to get them going. Some behaviors are more easily established than others, however. For reasons unknown, negative behaviors appear to become firmly entrenched after one trial. Positive behaviors seem to take much longer. The need for consistent reinforcement to establish a new behavior was brought home to us very clearly as we got to know our younger dog. She is a chocolate labrador who had been lovingly raised by one of our daughter's friends, but her lifestyle simply did not mesh well with owning an active dog who required a lot of exercise. So we adopted her when she was close to two years old. Our old guy has been around a while and is quite comfortable with his job description, which includes "stay off the furniture." It became immediately obvious that *her* former job description had included "sleep on furniture" and equally obvious that, were we to come to some agreeable arrangement for cooperative living, one of us was going to have to change our expectations. There was, in this case, little discussion as to which one of us that would be. Therefore we set about the retraining. It was apparent that, for her to learn the "stay-off-the-furniture" rule, we were going to have to correct her each and every time she tried to do things the old way. Otherwise she would not realize that the rule was "*always* stay off the furniture," rather than "*sometimes* stay off the furniture," since not even the most simple verbal explanation could explain the subtle difference. It became even more apparent that the satisfaction she gleaned out of even a few minutes ensconced in the comforter on the bed was worth the humiliation of being told to get down once in a while. Thus, we learned to correct her at the very beginning of her thinking process about getting up on to the bed or the couch or the chairs—which, fortunately, in a labrador is not difficult to ascertain, since you can virtually see the wheels turning. At first, it was very time-consuming and required a lot of vigilance (as does parenting), but she has learned. Now, she will look balefully at us and put her chin on the bed every once in a while, but it takes little more than a shake of the head to cause her to sigh and to turn away. Our old guy raises an eyebrow and gives us a knowing look.

To maintain a behavior, it can be reinforced intermittently

This is the issue that gets us all almost every time. Once a behavior is established, we must reinforce it once in a while to keep it going. We can't take it for granted. If we stop reinforcing it altogether, it will die unless it is intrinsically rewarding for a child: that is, it feels good to do it, even if parents don't notice or comment. Reinforcing a behavior every once in a while is called a "random reinforcement schedule" and is the most powerful means of keeping it going. If we give reinforcement on the 25th trial, for example, we establish the pattern that one must produce the behavior at least 25 times to get some reinforcement. When I am asked by a certain relative if I would like another piece of pie, and I say "no, thank you" umpteen times, but eventually give in and say "oh okay, but just a small piece," I have clearly set myself and my relative up for a dance that we are destined to perform as many times as we eat meals together. The same goes for parenting responses to such situations as giving in to whining, badgering, threats and intimidation, guilt trips, aggression and so on. There are times when we choose to give in to keep the peace or when we choose to ignore a behavior. However, whenever we make such choices, we have to remember that we have just instituted a very powerful reinforcement schedule, which will take some effort to counter the next time we are in a similar situation.

Several behaviors linked together become a "chain" which then act as one behavior

The behavioral rules that apply to an individual behavior can also apply to a chain. An example of a chain is: come in from school, drop clothing all over floor, wear muddy shoes into family room, turn on TV, get yelled at, walk back across family room in muddy shoes, take them off in front hall, get yelled at, yell back, get grounded from the TV, pick up clothing, throw into closet, go to room, slam door. This "chain" then becomes one behaviour and forms part of the child's job description around "coming home from school." Interestingly, we, as parents or teachers, frequently link ourselves to the sequence of behaviors and become an integral part of our child's job description. Homework is one particularly common area. "Wait for Mom or Dad to rescue me" has often been the tacit understanding of many a child who is involved in a struggle evening after evening. The way to "break" the chain, or to establish the chain that we want, rather than the one that we don't want, is simple in concept, but sometimes a challenge in practice. We want to take the child's body through the desired chain of behaviors without interruption or intervention from us. Hence, with the first example of the muddy shoes, the solution is to have the child dress herself completely and go outside the door to start the chain from the beginning. With as little verbal or physical intervention as possible, we then take this astonished young lady, who now knows that her parents have completely lost their marbles, right the way through the sequence of: coming in, removing muddy shoes, putting them in the shoe tray, hanging clothes immediately in the closet behind the door, taking the lunch box to the kitchen and washing out the thermos, going to the fridge, getting a snack, going into the family room, turning on the TV, settling down to eat the snack and watching the show. This is known as "positive practice" and has a very significant impact on children. It creates the very important "body memory" and required sequence of behaviors. Even after the first, assisted-learning experience, some good positive verbal reinforcement will start the ball rolling and maximize the chance of the desired chain being practised. I knew one Mom who took a morning off work to establish an efficient morning routine, stopwatch and all. She kept her kids going back to bed, getting themselves up, dressing themselves, preparing themselves to leave for school—as often as it took to get it to a reasonable length of time (I think she said three times each). She said she never had to remind them again. She had only to get out her stopwatch and they were off and running!

Punishment is defined as anything that decreases the frequency of a behavior

In the behavioral literature, *punishment* is defined as something that decreases the likelihood of a behavior recurring, whereas *reinforcement* is defined as something that increases the likelihood of a behavior recurring. We can have *positive punishment* and *negative punishment*, as well as *positive reinforcement* and *negative reinforcement*, since *positive* denotes something that is given, and *negative* denotes something that is taken away, and not how the child or we feel about it. Thus, *positive punishment* would be giving something to a child that results in a decrease in frequency of the behavior, for example a verbal rebuke that stops her from hitting her brother. A *negative punishment* for the same behavior would be taking away her freedom (e.g., by using a time-out) in order to decrease the likelihood of her hitting her brother again.

By contrast, to utilize reinforcement, we have to talk in terms of the behavior that we wish to increase—that is, a behavior that is incompatible with the undesirable behavior. This is the hard part, and is equivalent to the positive job description. We have to describe the behavior we want to see *increased*, in this case, playing nicely with your brother. Then we can give something to increase the likelihood of the behavior occurring (e.g., words of approval, token reinforcers such as stickers, etc.). This is positive reinforcement. Alternatively, we can take away something that increases the likelihood of the behavior occurring (e.g., we can terminate a grounding on condition that the desired behavior occurs, we can remove the telephone to increase homework-oriented behavior, and so on).

To illustrate these a little more clearly, the following table gives some examples of the various types of "discipline" techniques.

Examples of positive/negative reinforcement/punishment

	Positive (giving something)	**Negative** (taking something away)
Reinforcement *(to increase the frequency of a given behavior)*	stickers, candy, praise, thinking time, encouragement, money, approval, "lines" (I must…), rehabilitation… **"so that you will…"**	stop nagging; removal of distractions, privileges, freedom, company, approval, affection… **"so that you will…"**
Punishment *(to decrease the frequency of a given behavior)*	spanking, nagging, yelling, time-out, "lines" (I must not…), extra chores or duties, community service, prison sentence… **"so that you will not…"**	privileges, freedom, company, approval, affection… **"so that you will not…"**

While this may sound complicated, and it is rather, it is very important to understand the differences in order to analyze why certain situations work well and others do not. *It is also important to know that we can indeed discipline without punishment once we are looking at increasing desired behaviors. It is very difficult to discipline without reinforcement.*

The likelihood of any reinforcement or punishment working is increased when it is put into effect as soon after the original behavior as possible

Again, we turn to the dogs for a good example. By the way, I am not for a moment suggesting that we treat our children like dogs—just in case you were tempted to quote me out of context. I am merely noting that there are lessons to be learned…In this instance, I am referring to a situation where, for example, we come home to find a large and suspicious hole in the back yard. As a dog is, as we have already observed, relatively non-verbal, it is quite difficult to recreate for him in his head the precise situation as it was when he was actually digging the hole—how he was feeling, how good the earth felt against his paws, how the sound of falling clods and the joy of lying in the fresh, damp, cool mud broke up the general monotony of the day. Instead, we have to rely on his understanding that a certain tone of voice, a certain feel to the hand on the scruff of his neck, can create an atmosphere in which he realizes that he has done something wrong. Given his learning patterns, he may well grovel at this point, grimacing appropriately to indicate contrition, and roll on his back in humble submission. If we think he is responding to the hole-digging or to his general feelings of guilt at having ruined the carefully tended sod, we are sadly mistaken. He genuinely feels badly that we feel badly and that's it. Children are, indeed, not that different. We must catch them doing the good stuff and make sure we cash in on their (and our) feelings and thoughts at the time, and to catch them doing the bad stuff for the very same reasons. We may lose the moment if we wait too long. A notable exception to this is when we are really angry and act impulsively without giving ourselves time to think. If we can catch ourselves, it is sometimes better to take a cool-down period before deciding what to do, although the child needs to know that we noticed. We can, for example, let an older child or adolescent stew for a while, anticipating the worst, as in "I see you had some friends over for a party while we were away, even though we gave you strict instructions not to. There will be some consequence for this, of course. I'm going to think for a while about what they will be." In this case, we must be sure to follow up with something, even though many children will have volunteered some hours of "community service" in the meantime! Sometimes, with some children, we can even say: "What do you think the consequence should be?" Often children are harder on themselves than we would be on them. Following through is so important that it is wiser to go with the lesser of the two, rather than to agree with a child's harsher consequence, especially if we are unlikely to be able to carry it out—a fact with which they are sometimes only too familiar.

Compliance to a command or request increases when children are given a reason for complying

However, this is true only in children over the age of seven or eight. Up to that point, we are simply training ourselves to think of reasons for compliance and training children to expect reasons for compliance.

Copyright © 1998 by Baby Blues Partnership. Reprinted by special permission of King Features Syndicate.

Social learning theory states that learning takes place not only when we are ourselves reinforced, but also when we watch others being reinforced

This is known as *observational learning*, and means that children do not actually have to experience either the actual behavior or the consequence themselves; they can learn from watching others receive reinforcement or punishment. Observational learning can only be determined to have taken place once the child actually *demonstrates* the behavior. One of the main concerns of parents of young adolescents, in particular, is that by hanging out with the "wrong" type of child, our children will automatically pick up the negative behaviors these children adopt. In many instances, this will indeed happen. However, our children also see the results of these behaviors, and can learn vicariously that they do not wish to experience consequences. Just because I have seen someone rob a bank, does not in any way, shape or form mean that I will do it. However, I may see people rob banks and get away with it, or mouth off to teachers and get away with it. I may see someone become very popular because she has started to engage in a behavior that others appear to admire. In any of these situations, I may well decide to adopt that behaviour myself, until my own reinforcement schedule (whether positive or negative) is established. Although parents assume that negative behaviors are learned after very few observations, but positive behaviors take a lot longer, this is not necessarily the case. The impact of positive peer pressure is usually under-discussed and undervalued.

"I Don't Believe in Behavior Management"

Many parents and teachers freeze up at the thought of applying behavior management techniques. I have frequently heard such statements as "We don't want to get into any kind of reward system" or "We simply don't believe in behavior modification." What these individuals mean is that they do not want to treat children like rats or pigeons. They fear being caught in some token economy system, giving out points or charting behaviors in a rigid or formal manner, only to have children turn the system around to demand "payment" before agreeing to cooperate with normal, everyday expectations. They may have some basis for their concerns, since any tool, however appropriate it may be for some jobs, has the potential for misuse and abuse. We shall take a look at some ways that these techniques can work well later in this chapter, but first we need to look at the whole concept of behavior management, intentional or unintentional.

It is always worth taking a little time to consider that our whole lives consist of behavior management techniques in various forms. When I am giving a presentation, for example, I am encouraged by the nods and the laughs, and tend to wax ever more lyrical. When I have finished shopping for groceries, I go to the shortest line-up, since I have, on many occasions, been reinforced for equating short with quick, despite Murphy's Law that dictates that the one person in front of me has picked 95 percent of her goods with no visible price tag or bar code and is attempting to pay entirely in foreign coins. When walking home after dark, I tend to avoid dark alleys and less-traveled routes. In other words, I tend to repeat those behaviors that have resulted in a positive or pleasant outcome and reduce those behaviors that have resulted in a negative or unpleasant outcome.

Responding to a child's "Hi, Mom!" is behavior management, as is smiling at her joke, ruffling her hair, snapping a command, picking up her dirty laundry (or not picking it up), kissing her goodnight. In fact, it is extremely difficult to think of any social behavior that is not in some way involved in behavior management. We "manage" other people's behaviors; they "manage" ours. Thus is born social interaction and the reciprocal nature of parenting. Our children modify what we do just as we modify what they do. We also have some influence over the behavior of everyone with whom we come in contact. You may have heard the old groaner about "How many psychologists does it take to change a light bulb? Only one, but the light bulb really has to want to change." In the majority of circumstances, where others really do not want to change, changing what we do is the only option, and frequently one worth trying.

—•—

Jamie's parents claimed that they had tried everything to get her to comply. She had been absolutely fine until she turned four, three long months ago. Since then, she had become oppositional, defiant and just plain rotten. They loved her dearly, but had found that persuasion had its limits when it came to getting her to do things that she didn't want to do—which, these days, was anything and everything they wanted her to do. They did not believe in punishment or behavior modification, so had a pretty short repertoire of strategies. They had tried a form of "time out" where they had tried to persuade Jamie to go to her room for a while, but she didn't agree that this was a good idea. Once, Dad had tried to carry her to her room, but she didn't like that idea either and had fought tooth and nail, including kicking at Dad, which had forced him to put her down and think again. She was an only child and she was holding both parents hostage. She was desperately unhappy that she could not please them and they were not sure they even liked her.

Once both parents talked things out a little, they concluded that they really wanted to get their family back on track. It was first of all necessary to determine what behaviors, if any, Jamie already had in her repertoire that they wanted to see more frequently. In the midst of a crisis situation, there is little use trying to teach a child new behaviors. They put a blank sheet of paper with Jamie's name at the top in big letters on the fridge and agreed to monitor her for a week. Each time she did something that they found appropriate, they made a mark on the paper and made sure that she realized that they were doing this. They could choose to make the mark a star, a happy face, a check mark, whatever they wanted. They were to use as many marks as they possibly could, and to jot down beside the mark the particular behavior that they noticed. They were also to make a positive comment to Jamie along the lines of "good girl, you used your nice voice" or "good girl, you came when I called you." There was to be no tallying, no pressure, no coercion; simply a monitoring of the various prosocial behaviors they wanted to see. They were to bring the paper back to me the following week. They asked questions about what to do if Jamie insisted that they put marks on the paper, or if she ripped the paper off the fridge. They were told simply to tell Jamie that this was their paper, and that she could have one of her own if she wanted. They were also asked to give her a time-out for a few minutes as soon as she became non-compliant or defiant and not to wait until she was in the throes of a full tantrum. They were quite reluctant to do this, feeling that it was unfair to her. However, they agreed to try this for a week.

When they came back, the paper did not have an awful lot on it—just a few happy faces and a couple of comments about speaking nicely and doing as she was asked. However, both parents were amazed at how interested Jamie had been in the fact that they were putting happy faces on the paper and how she had immediately wanted to know why. They had told her that they were simply keeping track of all the behaviors that they wanted to see more, and she had been quite intrigued with the whole process. In fact, they had had such a reasonable week that they had almost forgotten to mark the behaviors down on the paper. They had tried a time-out sooner, and were concerned that she had simply gone to her room to play. We talked about the fact that this did not matter. The main purpose of the time-out was to remove her from the context in which she was becoming defiant. They went away with the suggestion to be slightly more vigilant in looking for the positives and to let Jamie end the time-out as soon as she was ready to tell them what she was going to do differently—whether this was five seconds or five minutes later.

They maintained the blank sheet the following week. It was filled with happy faces and stars by the time they returned. As with many children of this age, the monitoring alone proved to be a powerful intervention. Jamie had begun to understand in concrete terms how to please her parents and they had begun to define exactly what it is they wanted of her. Her behavior had settled down considerably and she was making a real effort to accumulate the happy faces. The early time-out procedure, with Jamie determining the end by telling them what she was going to do next ("I'm coming out now and I'm going to eat my snack," "I'm going to use my big girl voice," and so on), helped considerably. We had talked at some length about the need for her to decide what she would do, rather than simply to promise them that she would not do whatever it was she had been doing before. When we have a vacuum, we have a terrible tendency to fill it by doing whatever it was that had filled it before!

The natural consequence of all this was that both parents felt a lot more positive about Jamie after just a few short weeks. They were both willing to spend more time with her, reading to her, playing with her, taking her along on trips to the store or the marina. They felt that they had their lives back in control and that Jamie was definitely happier. And all this without any behavior modification!

——•——

The Positive Book

For those parents and teachers who can stand a little more behaviour management, the use of charts and communication books can be very powerful, provided they are used properly. There are a million tales of the communication books that get "lost" somewhere between home and school, and of teachers, parents and children who go through the motions without any substantive change in basic behavior. In many cases with which I have been involved, the children are left completely out of the loop, with little or no ownership of either the book or the behaviors contained therein. The book instead travels back and forth between home and school, rather like a daily report card, with the child referred to in the third person and increasing antagonism between the adult parties evident.

"Jon didn't bring his books home for his homework. I have tried to get him to do some math instead but he refuses point blank. He says he doesn't have any homework. Can you please clarify this?"

"The children in my class have homework every night. I have made every effort to try to remind Jon to bring his books home. I suggest that you have some consequence for him at home if he shows up without them."

"Thank you for your suggestion about the consequences for Jon. However, we are of the opinion that homework is something that he does for school and that it would be a good idea if you could ensure that he has the right books."

"I believe that it is Jon's responsibility to have his books and not mine to ensure that he has them. I have 28 children in this class, 27 of whom do not seem to have a problem remembering their books. Perhaps if he went to bed earlier and got more sleep he would have his mind more on his school work."

Get the picture? Even when a communication book does involve the child, it is my experience that it still talks about him rather than including him.

"Jon did not forget his books today."

"Jon finished his homework."

"Jon did not waste time listening to music or watching TV."

Notice the negative job description, or rather the suggestions that this list makes to Jon?

I think that most of us would agree that the mission statement here is to ensure that each child takes responsibility for his or her behavior—for monitoring it and eventually for internalizing it to achieve the goal of self-discipline.

The following suggestions are for optimizing the communication book so that the child gains and maintains ownership of his behavior. This approach, called the Positive Book, or as some have called it, the Success Book, relies on the concept of a positive job description and on the assumption that the vast majority of children wish to please the significant adults in their environment. It helps with self-esteem and is often not required for very long.

The **main purposes** of setting up the Positive Book are outlined below:
- to involve the child in monitoring his or her own behavior and in accepting responsibility for that behavior;
- to emphasize those behaviors that are desired, rather than those that are not;
- to replace *negative* self-messages with *positive* ones to address issues of self-image and self-esteem;
- to minimize the chances that the book will be "lost";
- to minimize adult involvement once the system is in place.

Instructions for Set-Up

- Have a meeting between parents or between parents and teachers to **decide what are the most important behaviors** to work on (e.g., completing work, focusing during class time, encouraging listening skills, reducing aggression, and so on). It is better to choose behaviors that are desirable both at home and at school.
- Try to pick **one major area** (e.g., social skills, task completion, classroom behavior, respect for others) and then pick **three or four specific behaviors** that are related to that one major area. For example, for classroom behavior, you could pick issues related to listening to instructions, starting work promptly, doing seat work independently, completing assignments, etc.
- **Be sure to include one behavior that the child will have no difficulty achieving**. This is to ensure a measure of success from the moment of inception.
- **Word each behavioral expectation positively and precisely**. Children

have a hard time understanding abstract generalizations such as "behaving well," "showing respect." They are far too vague. Try more concrete terms such as "speaking in a polite voice," "looking at someone when speaking to them," "taking turns," "waiting in line quietly" and so on. It is very important to choose behaviors that are incompatible with the behaviors that you do not want to see: for example, keeping one's hands to oneself is incompatible with hitting or poking; speaking in a quiet voice is incompatible with shouting; sitting nicely is incompatible with running around the classroom.

- **Sit down with the child to put the book together**. Either a parent or a teacher can do this. Make sure you explain that the purpose is to make sure you notice and keep track of the things he or she does right. The child may actually provide input in terms of behaviors he or she wants you to notice more. Try to brainstorm and take the child's ideas whenever possible, bearing in mind the general issues you want to include. Have the child illustrate the cover and the book if he or she wants. Older children may prefer to keep a simple spiral notebook or something lower key.

- **It is CRITICAL to this form of Positive Book to word each behavioral expectation as an "I" statement, not as a command or a comment, and that it be in the PAST tense**. For example:

   I sat on my chair all through French (NOT Jill will sit on her chair all through French).

   I kept my hands on my lap when I was listening (NOT Keep your hands on your lap...).

   I used my words instead of my fists when I was angry.

   I finished all the math I was supposed to do before recess.

- **Wherever possible, use words or phrases that are familiar to the child.** Avoid "adultese." For example:

   I kept my bum on the chair (NOT I sat appropriately).

- **Keep it very brief and to the point.**

- **Adding a comment about the child's feelings** can incorporate another dimension. For example:

   Even though I didn't want to, I spoke in my polite voice when I asked for something

   Even though I was very angry, I came when I was asked.

- **Divide the day into reasonable "chunks."** For younger children, or children with learning or attentional problems, it is important to make the intervals quite short, at least initially. Examples of time slots will depend upon when and where the behaviors are most likely to occur and the individuals involved. Possible divisions might be as follows.

  At school, nursery school, daycare:

  > before recess, recess to lunch, lunch to afternoon recess,
  >> recess to home;
  >
  > circle time, free play time, nap or quiet time, outside play time;
  > Language Arts, French, Music, Environmental Studies;
  > before lunch, after lunch;
  > before school, morning recess, lunch recess, afternoon recess;
  > bus to school, bus home from school.

  At home or at the baby-sitter's:

  > before school, before supper, after supper, bedtime;
  > breakfast, lunch, supper;
  > in the car, at the supermarket, on the way home.

- **Make sure that the child understands IN HIS OR HER OWN WORDS what the expectation is**. If necessary, you may have to catch her doing whatever it is and label it for her. "There, Jennifer, you are sitting and waiting beautifully! Don't forget to put that in your book later!"

- Set up a **box or circle** after each statement for the child to initial or check off.

- Arrange for the child to come to whomever has been in charge at the end of the time period, or to the homeroom teacher, or somebody meaningful, and **have the child go through the behaviors and check them off.** It is ABSOLUTELY VITAL that this is simply a run-through, NOT a reprimand, lecture, debate or punishment session, and that it not take up more than a minute or so.

- When you have run through the list, **make a positive comment,** even if it is stretching it a little, such as "Well done, two out of four today. Let's try for three tomorrow." **If the child is not able to check off any of the behaviours:** you may have set the goals far too high, so look again and simplify the behaviors or make them more specific; or the child may not be attending to his own behavior, so you will have to label what he did for him and help him check it off (e.g., "you sat very still all through circle time today, Ryan, so make sure you put a happy face here.") Remember to include ONE behavior that the child will have no trouble checking off, even if it something that everyone takes for granted. We once included "I breathed quietly" for a child with whom we had great difficulty finding anything much positive he could do!

- If the child marks off a behavior as achieved and you do not agree, **it is important not to make the child change his or her self-evaluation**. Explain gently why you do not agree and ask him to be a little more careful tomorrow before he checks it off. You might want to put your own check mark beside the child's if you agree, and leave a blank if you do not, although I would suggest that you do not unless you find it is absolutely necessary. It is very important NOT to write ANY negative comments. This includes "positive" comments with a sting in the tail, as in "You tried hard today, but could have done better." **Initial the bottom of the list** to show you have seen it.

- It is important that **NO SPECIFIC REWARD** be attached to these behaviors. The child needs to know that these behaviors are expected and that, when present, will generate approval from teachers and parents alike. It is, therefore, important to approve! A completely random, surprise reinforcer can be very powerful once in a while. For example: "You have been getting so many check marks in your Positive Book, how about we bake some of your favorite cookies?" or "What a terrific guy you've been this week! Why don't we have an extra story at bedtime?"

- Once a behavior is well-established, you may wish to **discuss with the child** substituting another behavior. This should be done with caution, making sure that the child realizes that you are not just trying to "trick" him or her, or changing for the sake of changing. You can try "You are so good at this now that we don't need to keep track any longer" as a way of introducing a change. Again, it is important to manipulate the list so that the child is ensured success. You may wish to extend the time period, rather than change the list of behaviors, say to twice a day rather than four times, or even to once a day if the child can manage it. It is unrealistic, however, to expect a child to behave perfectly for a full school day, especially if the child has an attention deficit or other behavioral difficulties. So please be willing to be slightly generous on occasion.

- For many children, it is helpful to add **"I was proud of myself today"** so that they can have a sense of pride in what they are doing. One little nine-year-old boy for whom the Positive Book had been very successful in reducing major aggressive outbursts was brought in by his distressed mom on a day when he had been suspended from school. I noticed that he had checked "I was proud of myself today," despite his behavior being such as to induce the suspension. When I inquired about this, he replied: "When I got sent to the office, the vice-principal went on and on, and I felt like hitting him, and I knew I should never do that, so I swore at him instead!" He kept his check mark.

Sample Positive Book

Jennifer T. DAY 1	Time 1	Time 2	Time 3	Time 4
Even though I found it very hard, I stayed in my seat.				
I put up my hand and waited to be asked before I spoke.				
I started my math when Mrs. Cookson told me to.				
I hung up my coat in my cubbie.				
I was proud of my behavior today.				

It is very important not to underestimate the power of the Positive Book, or of any other type of chart or reward system. Children's behaviors can change quite dramatically and rapidly once they realize that they can please others. It becomes very tempting to add a number of behaviors to the roster or to create even more charts, either of which may result in children being overly regimented and reacting negatively to something that had initially worked very well. On the other hand, we sometimes drop the reinforcement that the Positive Book brings a little too soon, and the undesired behaviors return. Many times, I have been told that the book did not work, when in fact it worked just fine. *Removing it* was what did not work. Some children need monitoring over a long period to help manage their behaviors; others respond well very quickly with the knowlege that they are pleasing significant adults, and this will sometimes be sufficient to maintain the desired behaviors. In general, if the Positive Book is not working, it has probably not been set up properly, so it is worth going back to the beginning and starting over. Hang in!

Chapter 10

Choices and Consequences

Free Choices—the Pitfalls of Parenthood

When we would ask my mother what she'd like for her birthday, she would always say "peace and quiet" and we would howl with frustration, realizing the futility of both the question and the probability of the response. "What would you like for breakfast?" "What would you like to do on your birthday?" "What would you like for Christmas?" The world of free choices and the pitfalls of parenting. There are actually parents who believe that they were put on this earth to fulfill their children's choices. I have met some who were desperate because they could not afford everything that was on their children's Christmas list and even more who were angry with their children for making requests that could not be granted. Children are not born knowing the limits of their choices. They learn them as they grow up and they learn them in many ways. Some children learn quickly, and make wise choices from very early on in life. These are frequently the same children who need only policies or values, rather than rules. They are frequently the pleasers who are attuned to the needs of others. They adjust their choices to suit the environment, and sometimes to increase the chances of getting their needs and wants met by understanding and manipulating the system around them. Other children learn by being told—by words. They learn their limits the same way. They may never actually have to experience the discomfort of the brick wall. They are told that it is coming and they learn to avoid it by choosing another, different route before they ever see it. Yet other children learn only by experience. They learn the consequences of their choices by living through them. These are the children who have to touch the stove to be sure that it truly is hot and fall off the climber to know that it really is dangerous. These are the children whom we tell over and over again, only to be tested and tested to see if we really mean what we say.

Parents are the children's initial providers of choices. We are motivated to keep everyone satisfied. Therefore, we fall into the trap of free choices only too readily. Sometimes, it takes an inordinate amount of time for us to learn that we set both ourselves and our children up. We find ourselves in the middle of a conversation with a 12-year-old that goes something like:

"What would you like to do on your birthday?" *[Free choice offered.]*

"I'd like to have the whole class over for a sleepover." *[Free choice made.]*

"Well, that's ridiculous, you can't have everybody over. What a zoo! Why don't you just have half a dozen of them over for supper and you could all go to a movie." *[Sorry, you guessed wrong. Unilateral suggestion made.]*

"A movie! Are you nuts? They'd all think I was a real loser. Jessica had a sleepover with everybody and HER Mom didn't mind." *[Response to unilateral suggestion. Return to original choice.]*

"But I'm not Jessica's mother and I cannot imagine why any sane person would let her 12-year-old daughter have boys sleeping over." *[True. But a no-win argument.]*

"You NEVER let me do ANYTHING I want to do on my birthday." *[Fighting words.]*

"If you talk to me like that, young lady, I can see you spending your birthday in your room!" *[More fighting words.]*

"Well, you ASKED what I wanted to do and you won't let me do it." *[True.]*

To retain some control over what we, as parents, feel we want to or need to provide for our children, and to allow children to learn to make choices for themselves, we can try to set up a situation in which we feel both comfortable and in control. As parents, we can attempt to offer a basketful of choices, and be able to live with whichever one our children select. We are in control of what goes into the basket, even when our children add to the selection we are offering. We can say yes or no to their suggestions and include them, or not.

Brainstorming is a technique used in a myriad of different settings. It consists of throwing all kinds of ideas into the basket, however ridiculous or far-fetched they may be. Everyone knows that this is just the first round and that the unworkable choices will be turfed out, either by the group as a whole or by the leaders of the group. Brainstorming in families follows the same rules, except that younger children or shy children or children who do not have particularly good ideas need parental protection from stinging comments by siblings. ("That's so *STOOOPID!*" is off limits during brainstorming, if not all the time.) Ideas for a birthday may include: a trip to Disneyland, a family outing, white-water rafting, heli-skiing, a pub crawl, staying out all night with friends, watching Monday night football with Dad, a Blue Jays game, tickets to an alternative rock concert, a class love-in, a night in a hotel with Zak Hansen, three friends over for cake and a sleep-over, a pool party, a tobogganing party, a party party. Those ideas that are too expensive, immoral, unsafe or just plain against family values can then be eliminated and the rest can provide the pool that is left in the basket.

Brainstorming is not always appropriate or even successful. Therefore, parents are frequently in the position of offering choices wherever possible. In other words, the safest bet for all concerned is to have a limited selection of choices, any of which is feasible, so that a child can feel some sense of freedom, particularly when there is some flexibility and some leeway. It is a basic rule of thumb to offer only those choices that we are willing to follow through—otherwise trust is broken and can take a long time to re-establish.

Hobson's Choice

In some instances, there is only one option and the choice may be to "take it or leave it." Many of us like to give our children a little more freedom. We wear ourselves out in this situation, trying to find some other alternative when our child does not like the one option available, rather than letting them take the other choice of "leaving" it. We start to cajole, persuade, beg, plead, grovel; then we get angry, trying to persuade our children to take the option we have offered:

"We are all going out for ice cream. Would you like to come?"

"You know I *hate* ice cream!"

"No, you don't. You LOVE ice cream. Come on, it'll be fun."

"But I want to go to Burger King and get chips."

"You have already had your supper. You are not *having* chips. Come with us and get some ice cream."

"You're only going for ice cream because Bobby likes ice cream and he only wants ice cream because he knows I hate it!"

"For goodness' sake, get your coat on, you're *coming!*"

Life would be simpler if we let our children experience the option of simply leaving it.

"We are all going out for ice cream. Would you like to come?"

"You know I *hate* ice cream!"

"Okay then, see you later!"

It is a fact of life that in some situations there is little or no choice. These are the non-negotiables, discussed at some length in the chapter on labor relations in my book *Who's In Charge?* Every family has its non-negotiables —situations where there are no alternatives to be found or where parents are not in any mood or position to provide them. Even in the most democratic of families, freedom cannot always be granted. Most children are not free to ride in cars without seatbelts, to take out a bicycle without a helmet or to run across a road in front of a speeding truck. Most of us have no difficulty with the idea that the car simply does not move and the bike does not leave the house unless the seatbelt or helmet is worn. While a handful of parents may still try to cajole in these situations, the result, in the absence of immediate compliance, is likely to be a rugby tackle or a tragedy. Much as we are reluctant to hurl ourselves at our children, few of us would not do so, given the horrifying alternative.

Zero-Tolerance Policies

Even within most non-negotiable situations, there is frequently some flexibility. It is important to understand the difference between flexibility and inconsistency. Inconsistency refers to the parenting team's failure to carry through on promised consequences, usually due to fatigue, laziness, or just plain burnout, with the excuse that "it's easier to say yes" or "it's much faster if I just do it." Parents then wonder why children don't trust the guidelines they have set. Flexibility implies responding reasonably to the situation at hand, always within the same policy guideline, and always with a positive decision to make an exception for a good reason. For example, a non-negotiable bedtime may be changed to accommodate a special occasion or a sporting event. When a child argues that it's a special occasion because there's a TV show he wants to watch, or because tomorrow is Tuesday, or because there's an "r" in the month, watch out! Flexibility is always accompanied by a reason that is in keeping with family policy, and its implementation is one of the requirements of the parenting job. Even with reasonable flexibility, however, children will temporarily believe that the particular guideline is once again up for negotiation; this must be clarified for all concerned. Too much flexibility may point to the need for a change in policy. No flexibility frequently implies rigidity.

However, various circumstances do require total rigidity. This is where zero-tolerance policies (ZTPs) come in. Many of us have heard about zero tolerance for violence in school boards, although this often manifests itself as mountains of paperwork and task-force reports, mandatory suspensions for Grade 1 children who get into scuffles on the yard, and administrators maintaining that they are unable to do anything about teens who carry weapons to school. Some principals feel that these policies are impossible to police and frequently give up before trying.

As a fierce proponent of non-violent conflict resolution, my views are understandably biased, and I acknowledge this bias up front. Over the years, I have had many discussions with colleagues who feel that children are naturally aggressive and that there is some danger in curbing these tendencies. This view leads to supporting and condoning rough play and the organized brawling that occurs in various "sports" as controlled expression of this underlying negative emotion. While I agree with the assumption of some natural, inborn aggression—I have often been bowled over by the innately destructive nature of some toddlers—I have a problem with the notion that we, as a society, must allow violence. We hear many an outcry around violence against women and other minority groups. Where are those who decry violence against men? In my view, we are unlikely to extinguish violence against women until we reprogram individuals to respond in non-violent ways, regardless of the gender or any other feature of the other person. Thus, wherever I can take the opportunity, I urge those adults responsible for child development to consider the imposition of a ZTP for all types of aggression.

The main assumption under any ZTP is that there is NEVER, EVER a good enough reason for the particular behavior to occur. Thus, there is NEVER, EVER any discussion if the particular behavior does occur. The behavior is quite simply NEVER, EVER tolerated. As with criminal trial, there are two stages: the determination of guilt and the imposition of a sentence. Thus, with a ZTP, there cannot be any ambiguity about whether the behavior occurred. Once this is determined, there may be some flexibility within the sentencing. However, there is usually a preset consequence for such behavior which can be modified only under exceptionally extenuating circumstances. For example, Barbara Coloroso supports a You-Hit-You-Sit stance to physical contact among even young children. In a ZTP household, this means that there is *never* a good enough excuse or reason for hitting your brother, no matter *what* he did to you or *what* sin he committed. Therefore, it is no use delaying the consequence or allowing any discussion. Whatever it was that prompted the attack can be dealt with at a later time, but the violence must have its own, immediate consequence if it is to be eliminated. The most successful way of dealing with violence is to make the consequence clear before it happens—as the child is thinking about it, if at all possible, or at the very latest as the hand is raised or the teeth are bared. Otherwise, the gratification achieved from a good thump on your brother's head can far outweigh the inconvenience of sitting out an afternoon's activities or being grounded from the TV for a week. Early intervention and zero tolerance can be successful in eliminating unwanted behaviors, provided they are used consistently.

"But we were only playing!" is a plaintive cry heard from many a child caught out in a potential violation of a ZTP regarding physical fighting. In families where aggression is a problem, even if with only one specific child in situations outside the home, a complete moratorium on any kind of fighting may be necessary until the problem goes away. While the distinction between "play fighting" and real fighting may be clear to some, it completely bypasses others. "It was a *accident!*" was one of our children's favorite expression for a while. Like most children, what she really meant was that she didn't mean whatever she threw at someone to hurt them when it hit them, or she didn't mean them to get upset, or she didn't mean to get caught. It is up to adults, both parents and teachers, to determine the boundaries for physical play for the children they are responsible for supervising, and to uphold these boundaries vigilantly. It is important not to be sexist and to decide that only boys need to be watched carefully for violence or aggression. Regardless of the child's gender, what many adults call "play fighting" is intimidation, bullying, coercion and just plain abuse in the eyes of others. This means that, in some circumstances, no play fighting can be tolerated. Believe it or not, children will still develop normally.

The amazing thing is that children become very familiar and comfortable with zero-tolerance policies when they see them being consistently upheld. In families, such ZTPs as no violence, always wear your seatbelt in the car, bike helmets always accompany bicycles, become a habit and they are rarely, if ever, questioned. While it might seem to go without saying that all family members, adult or child, are subject to the same ZTPs, especially where such issues as seatbelts are involved, there can still be two standards within the same family. For example, there may be a ZTP for children with respect to the use of alcohol or smoking, driving a car, using dangerous equipment, and so on, that does not apply to individuals over a certain age.

The reasons for ZTPs can be discussed openly as *they are being put into place*. Beyond that, there should not be much need for further explanation. Unless there is a serious developmental delay, our children do not need to be rocket scientists to remember that you wear your bike helmet whenever you ride your bike. Thus, ignorance of the law is no excuse. "But I forgot" does not cut it either. If the consequence is imposed, the chances of a child remembering the next time are vastly increased. If the child is simply talked at, the seriousness of the situation is undermined and the chances of the problem recurring are high. In a ZTP circumstance, the child has no choice.

Period. Thus, ZTPs are to be used with caution, care and consideration, primarily in situations where safety, morality and/or health are at risk.

No Means No

It is an unfortunate fact of parenting that "no" doesn't always mean "no." Sometimes it means "maybe" and sometimes it means "yes." This means that the word "no" cannot be trusted. Whether we are the parent of a young man or a young woman, it seems to me that we need to be vigilant to ensure that both genders know that "no means no"—long before they start to date or to form more intimate relationships. If we do not demonstrate this, how will they learn? The onus, therefore, is on us as parents to ensure that, when we say "no," we mean it. This means that we may have to stall and buy some time before we make a decision. "If you want an answer now, it's no" can be helpful in the familiar situation where we are called upon to make an instantaneous judgment. "Let me think about it and get back to you" is also useful, as is "I'm afraid you haven't told me enough about it yet for me to say yes or no." The half of the world that is decisive may have some difficulty with this concept, since the intuitive "no" is frequently also the reasoned "no." Thus, the spontaneous response is continually reinforced. However, recognizing that a "no" that changes to a "yes" encourages whining and badgering whenever a request is refused may help to persuade us all to think before we speak and to encourage debate and information-exchange before making a final decision. Knowing that another individual always means what he or she says is a remarkably solid foundation upon which to build trust and security.

Informed Choices

Prefacing many decisions with the words "You have a choice" can alert both parents and children to this fact. It should be noted, however, that even a simple choice can take many forms:

"Brandon, you have a choice. You can either put your toys away now or you can leave it till after supper." *[Genuine choice.]*

"Brandon, you have a choice. You can either put your toys away now or you can go to your room." *[Fake choice. Command in disguise.]*

By adding information regarding the consequences of the choices, we can give the child a fully informed choice.

"Brandon, you have a choice. You can put your toys away now and then they will be available to you the next time you want to play with them. Or I can put them away, in which case you will probably not find them very easily the next time you want to play with them."

"Brandon, you have a choice. You can either put your toys away now and life will go on as you know it. Or you can diddle around and miss supper."

Informed choices such as these are fair to both parent and child. Parents can quite easily follow through because they have given the child control over what happens. Parents are no longer the "bad guy" and children have a sense of empowerment. While it is never pleasant for a child to experience the more uncomfortable consequence of the two, at least he had the decision in his own hands.

Unfortunately, parents and teachers are both very good at messing up this simple and elegant learning situation. The following example is a little extreme, but most of us have been close to there.

———•———

Cory was a very talented, popular young man in Grade 7 at a junior high school full of wall-to-wall hormones—the school, that is, as well as Cory. He was, in fact, the star of the school's annual concert. Like most children of his age, he was occasionally struck silly, particularly in front of an audience of his admirers who were always delighted when he performed on cue. Sure enough, at the dress rehearsal to the concert, our Cory decided to indicate to the audience of his peers that he felt he was the Number One performer—gesturing to this effect with the middle finger of his left hand.

The music teacher was stuck in a dilemma, since her instinct to eject Cory from

———•———

the concert was tempered by the knowledge that, without Cory, there would BE no concert, as no one could replace him at such short notice. She wisely informed Cory that his behavior was unacceptable and left him to stew for a while, until she had consulted with the vice-principal—a wonderful lady with a good sense of humor and an appropriately thick skin, both prerequisites for venturing into a junior high school setting. The vice principal responded to the pleadings of the music teacher and called Cory to her office to provide him with the following, fully informed choice. He could rethink his gesture and behave in an appropriately sub-dued manner during the concert and the incident would be closed. Should he, however, decide to repeat this gesture in any form during the concert, he would be choosing a three-day suspension from school. Cory mumbled under his hair and left to ponder his choices.

The following day, in full view of a gym's worth of parents, teachers, school board personnel and various municipal notaries, Cory made his fully informed choice. Much to the delight and bated breath of his cohorts, he chose a three-day suspension which was duly and immediately granted to him.

Next morning, Cory's father, a lawyer, marched into the principal's office. In his hand, he clutched a sheaf of papers, including the school's behavior code and a number of statements of claim, which he waved in the air while he threatened to sue the music teacher, the vice-principal, the principal, the superintendent of schools, the director of education, and all the trustees of the school board, individually and severally, if they were to suspend his very talented and popular son who had done nothing that he could ascertain had contravened the behavior code or the law. As you can imagine, efforts on the part of the principal and vice-principal to explain that Cory himself had in fact made the choice to be suspended, fell on deaf ears.

Like every school trustee I have ever known, the trustees of this particular school board were acutely sensitive to their image, especially since it was election time—and Cory's father was a magnificent and powerful figure in full threatening flight. As foreseen by most of the lesser mortals in this scenario, and probably by you too, the predictable happened. The trustees felt that they had no grounds to suspend a talented and popular student whose misbehavior, they had to agree, was not specif-ically listed in the school's behavior code. Besides, they were not enthusiastic about having media coverage of a meeting at which they would be facing an articulate adversary of the Queen's Court. They crumbled and ordered the director of education to order the superintendent to order the principal to order the vice-principal to cancel the suspension, remove the letter from Cory's hitherto unblemished record and restore him to his classroom forthwith. They were reassured by Cory's father that Cory had learned his lesson from this experience.

That Darn Instinct Again!

While we may well have the inborn tendency to protect our children from any kind of discomfort, it is always very unfortunate when we get in the way of our children learning the real lesson we wish them to learn: that they can trust the world around them. When they push Button A, what we have told them will happen when they push Button A, will indeed happen—especially when we have gone to all the trouble of making sure that they understand the different array of buttons and their consequences, and when we have explained to them that they have a choice—if indeed they do. Our job, as the significant adults in their lives, is to make sure that they possess all the information they need to make the decision. Then we can leave them to it. They are in control of their own destinies, with our guidance and support; we will be there for them whichever path they choose. If we misinterpret this to mean that we must rescue them from their own, informed decisions, we do them no favors. If we merely threaten the consequences without letting them happen, we are setting both our children and ourselves up for a repeat performance, while they continue to test us to see if they can trust what we are saying.

If our children are still fairly dependent, and if the consequence of one of the choices we are allowing them to make is dangerous, immoral or unhealthy, then that choice should not be among the selection. Once our children are older teens or young adults, they will supply their own selection of choices. Our job may still be to ensure that we provide them with information that may assist their decision; thus, we take on the role of advisor or consultant, just as our parents did for us. While we, as adults, may seek advice from our elders and may even act on that advice, most of us would acknowledge that the choices we make are our own.

Teaching children to live with the consequences of their choices has to be one of the hardest parts of the job of parenting: watching Jon sit on the bench because he was late for the soccer practice after he chose to fight with his brother instead of getting ready; seeing the extra homework coming home because Diane chose to chat to her friends during math class instead of choosing to do her work; looking at the car sitting in the driveway because Ian chose not to put gas in it the last time it was used; seeing the embarrassment on Kristen's face when she took the makeup she had taken without paying for it back to the store. When we let these consequences happen, we may not have to do much more than let our children feel the discomfort and make the restitution. They will indeed have learned a very valuable lesson, and the chances are that they will not have to repeat it.

Fortunately, in exchange, we have the satisfaction of witnessing the positive consequences. We see our children smile as they read the comments on their report cards that show their teacher has noticed that they did all their homework themselves; we watch them take pride in the project they designed all by themselves; we notice the relief that they feel when they have made restitution for a mistake made at someone else's expense; we watch them mature as they take more and more ownership of each part of their lives and recognize that they are instrumental in shaping their own futures.

What We Learn from Dogs—and More

A dog's life—specifically that of the family pet, rather than a working dog—is fairly simple. Sleep, eat, go outside, walk, pee, poop, go inside, sleep, eat—or some minor variations on a similar theme. The dogs we have known have all been fairly grateful for being given a roof over their heads, food in their stomachs and the occasional scratch on the backside, together with being loved to death, of course. There are people who become quite perturbed when I compare children to dogs. If you are one of those people, you might want to skip this section. For those who are left, please rest assured that the comparisons are slim, at best, and that my children have never slept in a doghouse, been fed dry grain or been stepped on in the middle of the night. However, there are some very valuable parenting lessons to be learned from the canine world.

Since this chapter is about choices and consequences, we need to look at what we can learn from the simple choices that dogs can make and what they understand of the consequences of these choices. Dogs live very much by natural consequences. Our old dog, Max, a crossbreed, used to be quite a hunter, as most dogs of at least one or two of his various breeds probably are quite instinctively. Once, much to my consternation, he caught and swiftly dispatched a groundhog near a particular mound of earth on one of our regular walks. The neurons in his brain connected and formed a permanent pathway that said something like: "Go for walk; see mound of earth; run to mound of earth; find groundhog; dispatch groundhog; bury dead groundhog; watch while accompanying adult goes hysterical; go home." As far as he is concerned, this is simple cause-effect. The fact that he has never experienced a repeat appearance of said groundhog did not appear to dampen his enthusiasm for choosing to rush over to the same mound of earth countless times until some other neurons finally fired and he came to the conclusion that he had some other options. Fortunately, children learn a lot more quickly than this.

Like children, however, dogs learn primarily non-verbally, even though we talk "at" them a lot. The consequence of their actions must be close in time to the actions themselves so that they have a good memory of what they have done. It is even better if they are caught in the act. They learn from our tone of voice and our actions far more than they learn from the content of

Copyright © 1998 by Baby Blues Partnership. Reprinted by special permission of King Features Syndicate.

our words (i.e., something as opposed to nothing). They learn from what *happens* to them after a decision, rather than from what we tell them will or might happen. The moral of this shaggy dog story is that, regardless of what we say, what choices we offer, what decisions we guide, what lectures we give, what reasons we provide, our children will learn from what they *actually* see and what they *actually* experience.

Causes, Consequences and Conscience

Do dogs develop a conscience? Do children? Children certainly are not born with a conscience. Children, like dogs, are quite definitely born seeking the pleasure principle—if it feels good, do it—and seeking to maximize their own comfort level. A conscience has to be taught. Both our dogs clearly recognize when they have done wrong, but only after they have been taught that whatever it was they did was wrong. They understand that we are upset with them and that they are out of favor, at least for a while. Max has his guilty face when he knows he has done something wrong. His floppy ears are pulled back and flattened down; his chin is lowered and he gazes up from under his eyebrows so that the whites of his eyes are visible. Gallen, the young one, has a silly grin on her face, a sidle to her walk and a tentative wag to her normal weed-whacker tail. If the same response greets the same action over the course of time, they will gradually acquire some self-discipline and "feel badly" enough that they will not do whatever it was that caused us displeasure. They are both very sensitive to any softening on our part—watchful for the eye contact that signals re-engagement, responsive to the tactile reconnections of an ear rub or an absent-minded rub of the rump, alert to any change in tone of voice, and eternally grateful for any signs of forgiveness.

Children begin to develop a conscience when they are around five or six years of age, and this development continues for life. They start to understand that other people have feelings and that these feelings can be affected, both positively and negatively, by their behavior. They also learn that it is not a good feeling to upset other people, especially those whom you love and who love you, and most specifically those people you are terribly afraid might abandon you. It is this very discomfort that motivates the inner "policeman" who governs our lives from that moment on—the boundaries we set ourselves and seldom cross, or at least feel badly when we do. Children who are not permitted to feel this discomfort do not develop the sense of guilt or remorse that will serve to keep their own behavior within reasonable limits. Children without remorse are chilling indeed and are beyond the help of even the most skilled parent or therapist.

Much as it may seem to go against the grain of protective parenting, it is essential that we help our children to develop a conscience. Those parents who feel they were raised on a "guilt trip" have a particularly hard time with this. They usually vow never to make their children feel guilty about anything. Also, those children who have been raised to feel responsible for adult actions and behavior (such as children who have been abused) may well have some difficulty sorting out when it is appropriate to feel guilt and when it is quite definitely not. They will probably need some assistance to do this. Finding the balance between what our instincts or drives tell us to do and what is acceptable in the family and in the society in which we live is a life-long quest—what Freud would have called "ego development"—and requires some guidance and some accumulation of experiences.

Like the dogs, young children judge the seriousness of their behavior by the degree of negative response it provokes. If the consequence for each of their actions or choices is to be yelled or screamed at, or hit, our children will have an impossible task distinguishing between what is important and what is not. They will grow up in fear because of this. Most of us, as adults, have little difficulty understanding this concept. It is harder for us to realize that children who are uniformly exposed to a gentle "It isn't very nice when you do that" have an equally impossible task—if this is the response to everything from accidentally spilling some milk to setting fire to the house. Such children, who may superficially appear to be less disturbed than those who are continually berated, may actually be just as anxious when it comes to judging their own behavior.

Unlike dogs, children react to discrepancies between the words they hear and the pictures they see or the actions they experience. Such discrepancies create huge anxiety. I have met a number of parents who smile beautifully, all the while saying incredibly negative things about their child. I have met others who manage put-downs in the most friendly sounding of voices. There are parents who talk about having major surgery as if it were clipping a toenail while making a huge fuss about a child who chooses socks that don't match. There are parents whose expressions are so impassive, regardless of the emotion that they are feeling, that their children simply cannot read them and cannot, therefore, predict what is about to be expressed or what their response should be.

Both dogs and children need some of the same things. They need to be loved unconditionally, the way they are prepared to love us. They need warmth and affection. They need us to look them in the eye and to be open and as reassuring as we can be. They need a place to feel safe and nurtured so that they can explore their world and discover new and exciting places. They need natural, logical and consistent consequences for the choices they make so that they can learn to be accepted in their social world. Children also need to internalize our words, the messages they hear, so that they have accurate descriptions of themselves and their experiences, which help them to form a concept of self that they will carry forward into adulthood for the rest of their lives.

Chapter 11

Mirror, Mirror...

Building an Image

Of all the referrals for assessment or therapy that cross my desk in the course of a year—whether the main reason for the referral is for learning problems, behavioral difficulties, emotional issues, anger management, anxiety disorders or even giftedness—by far the most common concerns center on parents' perception of their child's lack of self-esteem. Believing that one's child thinks of himself as a "loser" or as "stupid" or as someone "nobody likes" tears at the heartstrings, and we yearn to change the world to be more accepting of each individual, warts and all.

The development of self-esteem, or self-worth, is actually secondary to the development of self-image (the mosaic of descriptors through which we define ourselves as unique individuals, different and separate from all others). Self-esteem, or self-worth, is the value that we place on our self-image. If we don't have a self-image, therefore, we cannot even begin to work on the concept of self-worth.

As I see it, one of my main jobs as a psychologist, is to find out what messages each individual client has received about himself or herself and the world in which each lives. We are all a product of the messages we have received over our lifetime. What we have built with these messages has formed the sense of "self" that interacts with our environment and all the people in it. This is our self-image. The more self-aware we are, the more we work on our self-image and the more we care about who we are. Also, the more we work on our self-image, the more self-aware we become. Self-awareness is not self-absorption, which is simply intrapersonal or within the self. It involves interpersonal as well as intrapersonal awareness; that is, how we appear to others and the impact of our selves and our behavior in the social contexts in which we find ourselves in life.

We start to receive messages as soon as we are able to use our perceptual abilities—our abilities to transform what we sense with our five senses (sight, hearing, touch, smell, taste) into meaningful experiences that involve some higher-level cognitive processing and memory. Even our so-called sixth sense, intuition, can be a conduit of the unspoken or unseen message into some form of storage. The problem is that, as alert as our senses may be, our ability to interpret messages that are sent is subject to some distortion. In many instances, the message received may differ to some degree from that which was sent or originally intended, since we tend to interpret new information in the light of information we have already stored. In addition, we may tend to discount any piece of information that does not fit our original mold, however compelling that information might be. It's rather like having a huge mailbox labeled "Original Perception" and a garbage can into which we toss any pieces of data that do not fit the label. Thus, if we think of ourselves as "fat," for example, a comment such as "Boy, you're looking healthy! Have you been away on holiday?" is likely to be interpreted as "Wow, are you looking porky! You must have been stuffing yourself on all-you-can-eat buffets for the last couple of weeks!"

Children are particularly susceptible to the messages they receive because they are essentially working with a blank sheet about who they are and how they fit in the world. Although seeking an original, adult-oriented identity is one of the primary tasks of adolescence (the other being the search for independence), the foundations for self-image are formed way before this stage of development. Younger children are like sponges, absorbing all that we tell them—not because they are actively forming the basis of their adult selves, but simply because they absorb all that we tell them. They act on what we tell them, because we all act on our perceptions of reality. As parents or teachers, we give our children messages a lot of the time, whether we intend to or not. Sometimes we do this directly: "You have such lovely eyes!" "You are such a ray of sunshine!" "You are turning into a handsome young man. You look just like your father!" "You are always the last one to finish supper.

Hurry up!" "You had better bring your math over here so I can help you. You have such a hard time when you try to do it by yourself." Sometimes we do this indirectly. "Oh for goodness' sake, let *me* do it!" "I guess that a B isn't too bad a mark when you consider how little work you put in." "That shirt is a wee bit tight for someone with your shape." "I always feel so comfortable when you're around." "Mom, guess what Jason did today? He cleaned up his toys all by himself! Jason, come tell Grandma all about it!"

The Birth of Self-Esteem

Once the image is taking shape, we begin to attach value to our various characteristics. This is the birth of self-esteem. Children will learn to value what we, their parents, value—at least for the first decade or so of life. Once young adolescence is reached, they tend to value what their peers value; and almost overnight, a comment from a parent becomes the kiss of death. Many of us have witnessed a young teen turn on her heel and change outfits after a comment as deadly insulting as "You look nice tonight" falls from a parental mouth. Similarly, "He seems like a nice young man" has probably ended more teenage romances than "Who was *that* underneath all that hair?" The same characteristic, therefore, that was seen as positive at one developmental stage may be viewed quite negatively at another.

© Lynn Johnston Productions Inc./Distributed by United Feature Syndicate, Inc. Reprinted with permission.

Whether we mean to or not, we sometimes place unreasonably high value on characteristics that are measured by children's report cards. I have met many children over the years who seem to exist in their parents' eyes only by virtue of what their teachers say about them; and any characteristics, skills or abilities that are not measured on the report card somehow do not seem to be valued in the family. This is just as true of families with professional, highly educated parents, as it is of families where the parents themselves never completed high school, but are bound and determined that their children will. It can sometimes be an uphill battle to encourage such parents to recognize and value such characteristics and skills as sensitivity to beauty, love of the outdoors, kindness to animals, ability to relate to the elderly, sense of humor, people skills, ability to do magic tricks, sense of justice, appreciation of inner peace and all manner of other non-academic strengths.

We know that self-esteem can be experienced in a number of different areas of a child's life, most notably athletic, academic, social and personal. While individuals with generally strong self-esteem would probably rate themselves highly in all areas, many of us who are more realistic and self-aware might well realize that we have our strengths and weaknesses. With maturity, we begin to realize that having weaknesses does not necessarily mean that we are weak. So we learn to accept ourselves in a more realistic light. For example, when I say, "I am totally useless at golf!", those who know me know this to be true. My friends might mutter little condolences to try to make me feel better; my best friends would agree totally. In my own family, speaking of one's accomplishments was considered to be big-headed, which was about the next to worst sin a body could every commit. At least, that was my impression. Thus, any pride one had in a success or a victory had to be tempered with self-deprecation, humor and/or external attribution to luck, the right weather, other people's mistakes. Yet, I seemed to grow up with a somewhat exaggerated sense of self-esteem. I was under the constant impression, for example, that I always got good report cards. I must say that the marks weren't all bad, but, when I read my report cards again, I realized that they were full of such statements as: "Margaret must remember that a leader must practise self-discipline in all things and by her example be an influence for good in the class"; "Margaret is an enthusiastic and energetic member of the class; I think more of her energies could be put to good use in learning her work more thoroughly"; and the classic "It is a pity that the standard of Margaret's behaviour is not up to the standard of her work. It is quite time that she became a more reliable member of the class." Back then, I read my teacher's handwriting as 'true' rather than 'time' and could not understand why on *earth* I was sent to the headmistress with this report card. I seriously thought it was because my marks were fairly respectable until I got there and saw her face. "She is always ready to find fault but should look at her own shortcomings first of all. As an ex-vice captain she should be most punctilious not to talk during 'silence' periods, to get ready for lessons quietly and quickly and to help in the smooth running of the class—not hinder." And *I* thought I was King Tut. I was actually 13. Say no more. This just goes to show how far from reality we perceive ourselves. I must say that a number of the comments are still disturbingly accurate.

Research shows that academic success is the cornerstone of self-esteem for children of elementary school age. This underlines the need to take special care in the school system to set up learning programs that foster the chances of success. If we placed emphasis on ensuring that children learn what they are supposed to learn, whatever effort or modifications the adults have to make, and if we were able to set individual, rather than group, goals for learning, we should perhaps all be better off. In an ideal world, this might happen. Children who excel in athletic activities usually have positive self-images. Those whose performance is weak, do not. Even though girls tend to drop out of athletic activities at alarming rates in early adolescence, those who remain retain their high levels of self-esteem, while those who choose to abandon athletic pursuits may find compensatory value elsewhere. Boys who excel athletically seem to keep their positive self-image well into adulthood. Socially, self-esteem is very fragile. There is a vast difference between popularity and having friends, with the former frequently being fleeting and susceptible to the winds of change, and the latter being a little more enduring. We are all, however, very well aware of the Terrible Triads—the threesomes of girls who cannot maintain an equilibrium of friendship, especially in the face of being asked to pick a partner for a school project. Friendships that are made or broken overnight are commonplace in the elementary school years; these can affect self-image and self-esteem in immeasurable and unpredictable ways. In adolescence, our children are frequently required to choose between us, their parents, and them, their friends. When pushed to the wall, they will more commonly choose their friends. Parents will still be around if they are not chosen, friends will not. This can be a tough time for us all, made tougher if we take their choice personally.

Personal self-image is so difficult to measure. There are few, if any, of us who can honestly say that we like everything about the way that we look. Body image issues are paramount in many young adolescent girls, primarily because of society's standards of acceptability as portrayed by Madison Avenue and Hollywood. As one magazine put it, of all the billions of women in the world, only a handful are supermodels. Yet many of our young women (and some older ones) strive for a perfection that is simply an illusion. This is another example of the power of the media; and we must do whatever we can to place these messages in the proper perspective. It is also an area where we need to reassure our children that they are beautiful to us, whatever they think they look like, just as we need to reassure them that there are no monsters under the bed or robbers hiding in the cupboard. They may not quite believe us, but they sure need to hear it.

Taking Back the Messages

Self-esteem is arguably at its most vulnerable in the preadolescent and adolescent years. This is when the more permanent self-statements that will provide the blueprint for adulthood are being formed. It is important for us as parents and teachers to listen for the messages our children have received and will now start to internalize, before they become too cast in stone to change. This is so that we can attempt, at least, to take back some of the messages that do not appear to match the reality. This process is a tricky one and one that tends to conflict with the process of listening to our children and their feelings.

When a child says: "I'm such a loser! I don't have any friends and the teachers hate me," we are told to reflect the feelings and validate them. "You feel quite unhappy about not having friends and you feel that your teachers don't like you." Now what? If we say what we are thinking, which could either be "Don't be ridiculous! The telephone rings off the hook. You're out every night at parties and your teachers voted you Teacher's Pet of the Year!" or "It's no wonder that nobody likes you if you behave outside the house the same way you behave here!" we are dead meat. In the first instance, we will probably be accused of not listening and not understanding. In the latter, we will probably be accused of not listening and not understanding. The picture is beginning to form, no? We can always mutter something positive like: "Well, Mom and I both happen to like you and we're pretty picky" and hope to get away with having to put up with sighs and rolled eyes.

Many children, in fact, throw out comments like: "I'm such a retard," "I'll never have any friends," "Nobody wants to play with me" and so on, to test the response. Not that this is a conscious process; it is simply an experiment to see what they get back. If our children are sponges, absorbing everything that they are told, we are mirrors, reflecting what we hear and see. If we reflect the negative messages, we reinforce them. If we can reframe them into positive terms, we can sometimes improve our children's self-image.

Many personality characteristics have both positive and negative aspects. A child who is stubborn is persevering. A child who is mouthy is not afraid to express an opinion. A child who is hyperactive is full of energy. A child who is nosy is curious about his world. Whenever possible, we can try to find the positive end of the continuum, or the other side of the same coin, and encourage that particular trait. The fact that parents often do this quite intuitively is the same reason that it is sometimes quite difficult to make parents see that their child can be a pain in the neck to others. A teacher who is worn down by a seven-year-old's inability to attend or sit for more than ten seconds at a time may not be particularly impressed with the notion that he is simply full of energy. However, it is important to understand that we need to find some way to reframe the negative message so that the child can find something in himself to value.

Parents who believe in equality among siblings, often have particular difficulty maintaining a balance in the family when it comes to expressions of self-worth. Children whose self-esteem is perceived as being *overly* positive and who are not shy about expressing it, may be the target of criticism from adults and other children. This may be constructive if it prevents a child from being labeled a "show-off" or conceited, since such children may have difficulty in some social situations with their peers, if they are perceived as overly pushy. It may, however, be destructive if it causes him to hide his light under a bushel. There are people, including parents, teachers, coaches, peers, and others, who feel that such children must be "taken down a peg or two." Because of this attitude, many develop a sense of shame or guilt because of their abilities or attributes. Some children are discouraged from developing their gifts or talents for fear of overshadowing brothers or sisters. Some children feel they must hide their positive characteristics when they have siblings who suffer from disabilities or disorders of any kind. They tread a fine line. Parental intervention may be required to maintain a healthy equilibrium.

The Self-Fulfilling Prophecy

One of the major problems in the area of self-image and self-esteem is that we are frequently stuck with reputations and perceptions that are developed quite early—and these become part of the world in which we live. Making changes, therefore, can be difficult and can affect other individuals than the one who creates the original concern. When working with families, we must always exercise caution when attempting to make changes in one individual (a child, for example) that will affect all family members. Negative behaviors frequently have a purpose, such as making sure the parents communicate with each other, making sure the child is noticed and parented, keeping the family together, avoiding major marital issues, and so on. Working on and changing the initial concern, however negative and destructive that behavior, characteristic or attitude may be, can sometimes reveal other issues that were not the primary reason for seeking assistance.

———•———

Amanda and I first met after I had spoken several times with her parents. She was 12 years old and initially seemed to me to be one of the most spoiled children

I had ever encountered. She had sat out in the car while I had seen Don and Daisy, refusing to come in, despite various degrees of bribery, coercion and outright threat to try to persuade her. I think her curiosity finally got the better of her. When she eventually entered the building, she was certainly a very unhappy camper, scowling from under her hair, spitting venom whenever she opened her mouth and treating both her parents with nothing short of utter contempt. Her first words to me were "I'm coming in, but I'm not going to talk and you can't make me." According to the reports from school, she was at least consistent. She was doing poorly academically, primarily because she never did any work, and was constantly rude to every adult in sight. Don and Daisy were both extremely concerned, although Don could not really understand why he had to take time out from his busy law practice to come to the sessions. Parenting was generally his wife's job; he was far too busy earning money to support the family. Daisy also worked, but at a low-paying sales job that she didn't much like. They had only the one daughter. They had waited many years to have this child and had been unable to conceive the brothers and sisters they had planned would join her. And to be perfectly honest, neither of them liked her much. This was not hard to believe. I must admit, I didn't much like what I saw either.

The temptation to take part in our discussions eventually grew too much for Amanda, and she started to interject comments, even though she was lying down on one of the couches with her back to the rest of us. It became clear that she may well have had a number of good points to make, but it was almost impossible to concentrate on the content of what she was saying, because she spoke only to interrupt her parents, still refusing to answer any communication addressed directly to her, and because of the sheer poison with which she seasoned every comment. I was not as surprised as I might have been when she agreed to come back for a session all by herself, as long as "they" weren't going to be there, especially "him."

Over time, I came to know a very different Amanda. This new one was actually quite shy and defensive. Although I had initially doubted it, she possessed a melodious speaking voice and a beautiful smile, and when she came out from under her hair and switched off the scowl, she was a lovely young lady. She sparkled when she talked about some of her own interests—art, music, drama, swimming—even though, she assured me, she "sucked" at all of them. She also confided that she was fed up with everybody saying that she should do better in school. She knew she was stupid and so couldn't do any better. This is why she had decided not to do the work at all. Her teachers were "all idiots," and what she was being asked to do was "ridiculous." She was fed up with being punished at home (grounded from friends, phone, TV, video games, CDs, all privileges in fact). The only way she could get any privileges back was to have an average of at least 75 percent on her next report card, which was several weeks away. She said, quite rightly, that her parents had nothing left to take away, so now she could do just what she wanted. She also confided that they had been considering sending her off to a private school, but when they did, she would just run away. So Amanda had decided not to care.

After some careful checking to make sure that she was still eating and sleeping properly and that there were no other signs of a major clinical depression, we took a closer look at her image of herself. On a self-esteem word checklist, she circled: angry, ignorant, disruptive, liar, forgetful, unsure, obnoxious, fat, ugly, tough, dumb, and lonely. "See," she added defensively, "I'm certainly not rude or mean the way my parents say I am."

In the next session with her parents alone, we explored the source of some of Amanda's messages. Don admitted to having a very short fuse and to being impatient in general with people who did not pay attention to detail. He was a Type A, driven perfectionist from a family where he was also an only child. He was an "absentee" manager, tending to dictate the rules for Amanda but leaving the implementation almost totally up to Daisy, then becoming somewhat frustrated with both his wife and his daughter when the inevitable conflicts arose. His own father had died when Don was only eight years old, and his mother had become a very busy, anxious, distracted, working mom who seemed to Don to have been constantly overwhelmed and to have little time for nurturing. He reported that he had had to take care of himself and swore that this had been very good for him. He seemed to love his daughter dearly, or at least he wanted to, but he was clearly and openly very disappointed that she did not live up to his expectations. He sincerely felt that she was a very bright young lady who should be having no difficulties in school, and that a 75 percent average was quite a compromise from what he felt she should be able to produce. He was also somewhat in mourning for the little girl who had adored him and for the young teenager he wished he had. He found it extraordinarily hard to talk about Amanda in anything but negative terms—and was quite surprised to hear some of his more critical, negative comments reframed to reflect a more positive aspect of the particular trait in question. When asked to describe her using the same self-esteem checklist that Amanda had used, he circled: angry, disruptive, forgetful, tense, obnoxious, lively, intelligent, jealous, rude, mean. As if to soften the blows, he added "occasionally" and "from time to time" to a couple of the less flattering adjectives.

Daisy, on the other hand, appeared to have spent most of Amanda's life trying to make up for her husband's negativity. Although the marital relationship appeared to be quite solid, she found it hard to follow through with many of his parenting rules because she either did not agree with the rule in the first place, or did not feel that the punishment or consequence was appropriate. Thus, she admitted to being "much too soft on her" and readily acknowledged that there was a high degree of inconsistency in how Amanda was treated at home. One of the main results of this inconsistency was that Amanda was quite confused about what her limits were. Therefore, she pushed them all the time, generally finding that they stretched and stretched until something snapped—usually her father—at which time the wrath of Don would be quite something to behold and dire punishments would be meted out. The adjectives that Mom felt best described Amanda were: forgetful, proud, depressed, anxious, sad, withdrawn, intelligent, emotional, tough, lonely, and fearful.

This was not an easy situation to resolve. There were multiple issues to be explored for each individual: why Daisy found it so hard to set limits and be consistent; how Don could learn to love when he had not felt loved as a child; how to help Amanda in school; but most of all, how to turn around this very negative situation so that Amanda's self-image would change and her self-esteem would become positive. However, all three individuals felt that it was worth a try.

It took a while, but finally Amanda began to enjoy coming for the sessions. She basically learned how to use what we called her "sucky" voice to put her points across without the venom—although she always did so much better when her parents were not around. Her teachers reported that she seemed more settled at school and that she was paying some lip service to her work, although it was still less than adequate. It took some persuading to have them try to acknowledge each small step, and they did this between gritted teeth, but they bought in to the fact that this was the beginning of a long journey for Amanda and that she needed whatever encouragement they could muster.

It has been extremely hard for Don to change his approach with his daughter. He was a man who had been brought up to feel that he should always be competent, and he had a strong feeling that, because Amanda was so defiant and rude, he was not a competent parent. So he left all the parenting up to Daisy. He was somewhat awed by her compassion and her ability to feel positive even in the most negative situations, but had never told her so, and he became highly anxious when she needed his help. He started to explore some of his belief systems about himself and looked at his comfort level in ambiguous situations, or situations where he did not have complete control of the outcome. He was able to retrieve his sense of humor and started to be able to identify Amanda's to make some small connections. He tried very hard to make positive comments, even when Amanda rebutted them, or spat nails, or simply ignored him, and he fought his instinct to flatten her or to spit nails back at her. This will never be easy for him, but he is trying his best.

Daisy, on the other hand, needed to explore ways in which she could set limits for Amanda and stick with them, without feeling that she was being overly punitive or damaging her daughter in any way. She wanted to feel confident that this would be for Amanda's good and that she would not end up being the "bad cop" as Don had become. They were able to talk together about the need for parents to spell each other off and to support each other, without either one becoming entrenched in a role that was uncomfortable. She experimented with some choices and consequences in fairly low-emotional-content areas, such as doing laundry, and learned to wait Amanda out and to walk away from the verbal abuse. She became very comfortable with the idea of presenting the types of messages she wanted Amanda to internalize as she became an adult woman, even though we both knew that it would probably be many years before she ever knew whether this had worked. As she sent such messages as: "I deserve to be treated with some respect" and "I am competent and comfortable with my role," she reported that she started to feel better about herself, and was much more able to be strong when it came to carrying through on promises she had made to Amanda. She had no trouble at all with increasing the number of positive statements she made to her daughter and was much better than Don at keeping these up, regardless of the response received.

For her part, Amanda still says that her teachers are "idiots," that "school sucks," and that her parents are "losers," but she spends far more time out from under her hair and without her thundercloud look. She is beginning to discover that you can catch more flies with honey than with vinegar, and is learning that you can be more successful understanding the system and running with it, than tilting at windmills. The last time she completed her "positive" list, it read as follows: angry, active, responsible, forgetful, unsure, tough, lively, lovable and kind (to animals). She asked if she could add words of her own, and tacked on "realistic."

What Goes Around Comes Around

From Amanda's story, it became clear that parental self-esteem is once again an important variable. It is important for children to have role models who feel good about themselves—people who have a clear self-image upon which they place positive value. It is, therefore, necessary for us, as adults, to monitor ourselves and notice when things are not going right. This reinforces the need to make the effort to take time for ourselves in the midst of the job of parenting (ourselves as individuals and ourselves as a couple) to find what we are proud of, what we feel we accomplish, what makes us feel good. It is gratifying to discover that looking for positive characteristics and behaviors in our children and commenting on them can also make us feel good about ourselves. So even when things look bleak, it is certainly worth looking for opportunities to praise a child, however close to the bottom of the barrel we have to delve. The following list has been among my collection of trivia for some time. The original is from a journal called *Communicate,* Volume 7, Number 11, published in spring 1995, by Gary Kene and his colleagues. I have adapted it slightly, with apologies to the original author.

1. *Has a great smile*
2. *Loves pizza and so do I*
3. *Says please and thank you*
4. *Likes music and dancing*
5. *Has a good imagination*
6. *Is great at colouring*

7. *Brushes his/her teeth after meals/at bedtime*
8. *Is good at remembering people's names*
9. *Makes a great showman*
10. *Is a fast learner*
11. *Always tries hard, even though s/he may not get it right the first time*
12. *Has good manners when we're in a restaurant*
13. *Listens when I say no in a store and doesn't embarrass me by arguing in the store*
14. *Is good with the baby*
15. *Likes to help out*
16. *Sings lullabies to the baby*
17. *Likes to sing to me*
18. *Draws great pictures*
19. *Is truthful*
20. *Likes to share*
21. *Is learning to share*
22. *Is great at playing "I spy"*
23. *Feeds the cat and changes the litter without having to be nagged all the time*
24. *Likes to tell me about how his/her day was*
25. *Likes to make cookies together*
26. *Is my buddy; we have great conversations together*
27. *Tells good jokes and makes me laugh*
28. *Has beautiful eyes*
29. *Loves animals and is gentle with them*
30. *Gives great hugs*
31. *Loves being outdoors in the fresh air*
32. *Just looking at you makes me happy*
33. *Makes me glad to be his/her mother*
34. *Has fun*
35. *Plays nicely with others*
36. *Puts toys away*
37. *Tells me where s/he goes when outside playing*

38. Tells me when s/he is scared about something
39. Helps clear the table after supper
40. Respects elders
41. Has a great laugh
42. Helps dry dishes and does a great job
43. Helps and encourages brothers and sisters
44. Keeps his/her room tidy
45. Listens when told to turn off the TV
46. Likes to be hugged
47. Learns from his/her mistakes
48. Chooses own clothes for the next day
49. Plays nicely with younger brother while I'm cleaning the house
50. Is able to show concern for others
51. Keeps his/her room clean
52. Chooses nice friends
53. Ignores teasing and doesn't get into fights
54. Loves to curl up when we read out loud together
55. Has lots of good ideas
56. Is fun to be with
57. Likes to learn and is inquisitive
58. Plays a great game of Nintendo
59. Knows all of the players on the Blue Jays
60. Is careful with dishes, furniture, etc.
61. Behaves when we are visiting others
62. Likes school and teachers
63. Is helpful around the apartment, house, yard, etc.
64. Knows when to ask for things
65. Gets dressed on time in the mornings
66. Has good posture
67. Is polite on the phone when others call
68. Is good at singing jingles from the commercials
69. Uses his/her words when s/he is angry instead of throwing or breaking things
70. Doesn't name-call

71. *Does homework without much trouble*
72. *Wants to go with me when I have free time*
73. *Is generous and offers to share*
74. *Cares when I am sick*
75. *Makes my birthday special*
76. *Is good company*
77. *Tidies up when asked*
78. *Can be busy by him/herself and amuse himself*
79. *Is polite when I have guests or friends over*
80. *Eats breakfast/lunch/dinner*
81. *Knows her/his colours*
82. *Knows her/his ABCs*
83. *Knows how to spell her/his name*
84. *Doesn't cheat at games*
85. *Tells others s/he is glad I'm her/his mom/dad*
86. *Is a good reader*
88. *Is good at helping to put away groceries*
89. *Tells me when s/he spills something*
90. *Can dress her/himself*
91. *Is good at putting her/his coat on*
92. *Cleans up when s/he spills something*
93. *Says how s/he is feeling*
94. *Enjoys playing games with me*
95. *Knows whom to tell if s/he has a problem*
96. *Follows safety rules when crossing the street*
97. *Knows his/her address/phone number*
98. *Is both a good winner and a good loser*
99. *Knows correct foot when s/he puts on shoes*
100. *Knows that I love him/her.*

Little by little, stone by stone, year by year, we build the foundation upon which our identity is built. On a solid foundation, begun by nurturing parents, a child can learn to withstand the many onslaughts she will face over her lifetime. We need to be both realistic and reassuring with our children so that they will trust us when we give advice or praise or constructive criticism. We must continue to outweigh negative comments at least four to one with positive ones, even if we believe we are not being heard. It may be a long time before we see the fruits of our efforts. We must be patient. If we give up, our children give up. We also need to remember that we are not solely responsible for our child's self-image. She will encounter many other sources of influence and messages—both positive and negative—along the way. There are times when our constructive efforts appear to be undermined or even destroyed by a chance remark from another adult or child, or perhaps through consistently negative messages received from society at large. Our vigilance is necessary and our interventions can sometimes be therapeutic and positive; but ultimately our child-adult will form her own image of herself and test it against the realities of the world beyond the family. We will probably not be with her when this image is put through its paces. All we can hope is that we have done as good a job as we can while we had the fleeting chance, and that we can appreciate and continue to value what she has done with the raw materials she has chosen for herself.

Chapter 12

The Road to Independence

Born to Leave

Accompanying our children along the road to independence, keeping them safe and healthy along the way so that they can leave the family as fully-functioning adults, is the fundamental task of parenting. In other words, our main goal as parents is to do ourselves *out* of a job.

To prepare us for the complex world in which we live, the human brain takes longer than that of any other species to mature to its full potential. Thus, our offspring need more time to acquire all the necessary skills to leave the nest fully equipped for survival. We know that the human infant is an amazing machine, with a physical system that adapts to its environment; the second it is born, it is capable of taking over the task of breathing air, regulating its temperature, signaling when it is hungry or otherwise uncomfortable, activating its digestive and elimination systems, discriminating and processing light and sound, moving all its limbs, storing memories and learning from experience, and countless other skills that are essential to its survival outside the uterus. Yet, without the support of a competent caregiver, this infant will not survive. Our children start their lives completely dependent upon us in every sense and for every aspect of their existence.

The end of adolescence and the beginning of adulthood are when we can tell our parents that we can manage without them, and, by the way, thanks for bringing me up. While this is sometimes first expressed verbally around the age of five, if not before, it is not until we reach our early adult years that we can truly complete our quest for independence and show our parents that we can function fine on our own. Some of us never do. Cutting the umbilical cord or untying the apron strings is extraordinarily hard for many adults, as many a spouse or partner has discovered—whether that tie is there for love, fear, obligation, anxiety, self-doubt, or simply not knowing that we can. We have to change our relationship with our parents from being the child to being able to deal with them on adult terms: respectful of each other as human beings, perhaps never equal, but at least equivalent within our original family unit, and nonetheless separate from them. Until we have completed that particular task, it can be quite a challenge to be competent parents ourselves.

The Developmental Journey

The gradual process begins with the total dependence of the newborn infant and is completed with the declaration of independence at the end of adolescence. The road has many ups and downs, twists and turns, and some developmental signposts along the way to show us that we are on the right track. Provided they are not raised in an environment of deprivation, our children generally learn to crawl, pull themselves up and walk, and cry, coo, babble and utter single words, all within a relatively narrow time frame, and relatively independently of what we do as parents. We expect that, by the time they reach the age of five or six, they will have learned to communicate in a meaningful way, to use a toilet appropriately, to eat and drink individually, to sleep civilized hours and to socialize with others in a suitable manner. When they leave the nest, we expect them to be capable of total independent living: to have the education and skills to make enough money to survive, to look after themselves and their immediate environment, to stay out of trouble and to keep themselves healthy and safe. In addition, we may have the aspirational goals that they be literate, numerate, socially adept, content with themselves and capable of forming and sustaining the meaningful relationships that will carry them forward into their adult lives.

As parents, we have various important tasks to perform along this road. If they are to become independent of us, we have to move from doing every-thing for our children to letting them do everything for themselves. The route that we take to do this can best be described as a continuum:

0	1	2	3	4	5	6
doing	directing	teaching	helping	prompting	supporting	letting go

In other words, we begin by doing everything for them. We follow this by telling them what to do, by directing their behavior. Then comes the most important task of all—teaching—one which we sometimes do our-selves, sometimes delegate and sometimes wonder at where they learned what they have learned! As our children grow up and acquire more skills, we proceed somewhat erratically through the various steps towards inde-pendence, providing more or less support, depending on the needs of the individual child or on the demands of the particular task. At different stages of development, children can be more or less independent, even if it takes time. Any given child will, of course, be quite independent in some cir-cumstances and heavily dependent in others. Young adolescents epitomize this particular phenomenon, but even adults retain it to some extent. Most of us have heard the dreaded "ME do it!" from a two-year-old, followed almost inevitably by the tantrum if we insist on taking over because we are in a rush, or because it just isn't done *right*. Some children are born inde-pendent, others are quite content with servants all their lives. Different aspects of living have different degrees of risk. We can permit a two-year-old to experiment with independence in dressing herself. We can also allow some exploration of her environment, provided we make sure that she is safe. However, if, for example, we let her take over all the decisions about what she will or will not eat or when she will or will not go to bed, we risk her health and her safety. Thus, some of our classic battles begin. Most of us recognize very early that we have to give a little to get a little, and we start the process of teaching our children how to make choices that will not only be good ones in their quest for autonomy, but will also give them ways to please us along the way!

Discovery Learning

Although the Mythical Family has children who respond to a single, simple, verbal instruction, teaching children usually involves far more than telling them what to do, even if we repeat ourselves *ad infinitum*. In fact, this is a very small part of the process of learning. Children learn from watching. They watch us; they watch their siblings and their peers; they watch television and videos. Research has taught us that the media provide very powerful models, but that we, as parents, have the potential to be the most powerful. Fortunately or unfortunately, we do not know what our children are learning until they imitate the various behaviors in their inner repertoire.

Children also learn from discovering, from doing. Dr. Byron Rourke, a Canadian neuropsychologist who specializes in non-verbal learning disorders, tells the following story:

———•———

A three-year-old child is sitting in the middle of Aunt Gertrude's living room rug. She looks around and sees a beautiful, colorful vase on a small table at the other side of the room, glinting in the sunlight. She gets up and runs over to the table, picks up the vase and throws it up into the air. The vase reaches a certain height and then drops to the floor, crashes with a loud noise and smashes into hundreds of pieces. The child's mother, who is sitting on the couch, says: "That's Aunt Gertrude's vase!" In addition to learning the name of the object and that her mother is a source of information, this child has learned about planning and executing an action, distance, speed, the feel of the vase, gravity, force, acceleration, the structure of materials, and various aspects of the fragility of matter.

Another three-year-old child is sitting in the middle of Aunt Gertrude's living room rug. She looks around and sees a beautiful, colorful vase on a small table at the other side of the room, glinting in the sunlight. Her mother sees her looking at the vase and says: "That's Aunt Gertrude's vase!" In addition to learning the name of the object, this child has learned that her mother is the source of information, period.

The moral of this story is not that we should encourage our children to vandalize other people's property. It is that we cannot allow ourselves to be the sole source of information or support available to our children. This, the ultimate control, will not enhance their growth. Children are not empty vessels to be filled with words. They need to be *encouraged* to be active learners—and they will not do this simply by sitting still and being told. The education system has paid lip service to this philosophy for years as anyone who visits an average elementary classroom sees. However, the system sometimes tries to skip directly to the end of the continuum and children as young as kindergarten or first grade are left to drift aimlessly in a "child-centered" learning environment without leadership or guidance. Whether they ever discover anything worth learning is left entirely up to them. This is a cop out. It disregards the concept that independent learning, as with independent anything, is a process and not a sudden step-function.

One Step at a Time

Perhaps the best way to illustrate the intermediate steps in the journey towards independence is to look at a family where homework was a humungous issue. Judging from my conversations with parents over the years, you will probably think that this story is about your family and that I have been in your house. To my way of thinking, homework is and always has been a simple contract between a teacher and a student. I have always presumed that the teacher has a reason for assigning the work, and that the student has something to learn from doing it. Silly me.

—•—

Kelly was 14 years old and in Grade 8 when the family first sought help. Getting her to do her homework had been a problem for a number of years. The family was very big on education. Both parents were high-school graduates with post-secondary degrees and Kelly's older brother had always been what they described as a "good student. Kelly, on the other hand, had average marks, when she completed her work, although both her teachers and her parents felt that she was bright and could do much better "if only she tried." The main reason they were seeking an assessment and some assistance at this juncture was that Kelly's behavior was becoming unmanageable at home, ranging from outbursts to the silent treatment, and her teachers were concerned about whether she was ready to go on to high school the following fall.

It transpired that the evening routine in this family's home was an exercise in chaos. Kelly's homework time appeared to last from the time she came home from school to the time she went to bed, with a brief respite for food, and it was almost exclusively issues around school and school work that triggered the outbursts and other evidence of Kelly's (and her parents') frustrations. Both parents took shifts to "help" their daughter with her homework, and seemed to vacillate between groveling and screaming, passing through nagging, cajoling, pleading, begging, bribing and threatening on the way. By the time she was in bed and asleep, both parents were at each other's throats, if they were talking at all. This constant conflict had taken a toll on their relationship, and their relationships with their son, who retreated to his room or left the house almost all the time to get away from the noise. However, despite all this furor, Kelly's homework was, for the most part, done—and was taken back to school as an almost perfect finished product with little or no apparent signs of the warfare that it had engendered. Actually, what ended up being evaluated at school was primarily her parents' efforts, since they reported that they had to make her do it, and that they frequently ended up writing or typing up assignments, solving math problems, making her copy her work over more neatly, correcting her spelling, punctuation and grammar, and doing the library research, which she almost inevitably left until the last minute. Her teachers suspected that the work being returned was not Kelly's, since they saw little evidence of any consistent learning in her class work or her tests and exams. However, there were 34 students in the class, many of whom were disruptive and troublesome, and no one had the time to focus on Kelly. Sometimes they didn't even have time to go over the work they had given the children to do. At least, in Kelly's case, the homework was done.

Kelly's parents were quite surprised that the initial focus of our sessions was on them, since they had expected their daughter to be seen individually and her problems hopefully "fixed." Instead, we talked a great deal about their roles as parts of the family management team: who did what; who was the one who set conse-quences; who upheld them; what they expected of their children; what messages they had received from their own childhoods about what parents and children did; and what their philosophies as parents were. Then we focused on what they felt Kelly's "job" was at present. Predictably, they talked about school and how they were not particularly gung-ho on good marks, but they really felt it was important for her to put in as much effort as she could. They also would have liked her to be more involved in athletics or arts or music, but all she wanted to do was hang out at the mall with her friends and watch TV. It turned out that Kelly was pretty much grounded for life and was, therefore, not involved in anything at all. She had had all TV and telephone privileges removed into the foreseeable future and was not allowed out of the house except with the family on family occasions. At least, in theory. In fact, it turned out that some of these privileges were there some of the time, primarily, it seemed, when she made life so miserable for her parents that one of them would fling up their hands and say something along the lines of: "Oh, for goodness sake, ALRIGHT! Why should I care if you never get a job!" or the other one would feel sorry for her having been cooped up for several days in a row and let her out on parole. Kelly would then slip away and leave her parents arguing about things like consistency, or "jellyfish," or corporal punishment, and saying things like: "Don't you bring my mother into this!"

A psychoeducational assessment of Kelly revealed a slightly low average level of ability across the board with no particular learning disabilities or other specific problems that might have been interfering with her performance in school. However, during the assessment, it became clear that Kelly was an extremely pas-sive personality. She constantly waited to be told what to do, even if she was already familar with a particular task. The fact that she responded correctly when she was asked "What do you think you are supposed to do?" or "Do you remem-ber what you were asked to do?" indicated that this was not a matter of lack of basic reasoning or a poor memory. She also had a tendency to blame her tools if she was having any difficulties. "You didn't give me enough pieces to do this puz-zle," "Oh, I didn't know you meant…," "This passage is too hard," and so on. She looked for assistance constantly—everything from asking for help directly to searching for non-verbal cues on how she was doing—and frequently said "I don't know" or "Pass on that one," rather than trying to guess or work the problem through. Like most passive, dependent learners, she had a particularly hard time with math, since math requires a lot of active problem solving and some staying power. It seemed that Kelly had an acquired learning problem. Her parents were doing most of the work, while she had not bought in to the fact that she was part of the process at all! And she was a long way from being an independent learner.

Fortunately, her parents were willing to extricate themselves from the loop so that Kelly could begin to stand on her own two feet. As we predicted, she was very anxious at the prospect of trying things alone. So were her parents, perhaps more so. It was obviously too big a leap to throw her into the deep end of independence suddenly and hope that she would swim. Kelly and her parents were stuck on the scale somewhere between 0 (doing) and 1 (directing)! So the goal was to get at least to a 3 (prompting) within the next month or two, and then hopefully on to a 4 (supporting) by the end of the school year.

First of all, the "job" homework was defined and each party was allocated his or her own responsibilities. It was decided that it was each individual teacher's job to assign and to evaluate the homework that Kelly was given. Her parents gave the teachers their support for following up if Kelly had not done her homework or had not completed it satisfactorily, and so there were consequences at school if the job was not done properly. Fortunately, the teachers followed up with this part of the deal. Her homeroom teacher agreed to help Kelly initially to ensure that she had checked her planner before she left the school, although the responsibility for this task was to be handed over to Kelly within the month. Kelly's parents took on the responsibility of expecting her to work on homework for a set period of time five evenings a week (Sunday through Thursday). An hour per evening was agreed upon by Kelly, her teachers and her parents as being a reasonable amount of time to spend. The hour would not begin until she was fully prepared to settle down and work. Her parents were responsible for ensuring that she had a quiet place to work and that she was not disturbed by the telephone or otherwise interrupted during homework time. They also agreed to start the timer once she told them she was settling down and to let her know when the hour was up. The most important part of their agreement was to provide assistance ONLY when it was asked for, and ONLY if Kelly could tell them exactly what help she needed. "I don't know how to do this" would not suffice. She had to show them what she had to do, what she had done and where she had run into difficulties, and then she was expected to tell them what help she needed. They were to be "on duty" for a set shift of half an hour each during the hour that was set aside for homework. If Kelly did not settle down at the prearranged time, they would be off duty as expected at the end of their shift, so if she needed help later, that was too bad. They also agreed to sign her planner to say that they had seen it. They were encouraged to permit Kelly to be responsible for various aspects of her own life outside of school—for example, to do her own laundry, make her lunch, look after her room, take care of her own belongings, make supper once a week (Kelly's choice of one "community service" activity), and so on, so that she could acquire some useful skills before she left home.

We all did a little work together on the types of questions Kelly would have to have in her head to help her in situations where she found it hard to get down to work, and these were shared with her teachers. "What is it that I have to do? Do I have all my books? Did I write my homework in my planner? Do I need to ask the teacher anything before I leave school? Have I read the instructions? Do I under-stand the question? Can I find an example that I can look at somewhere else? If I don't know how to do this question, are there any others that I CAN do? If I can't do it all, can I at least do some of it? Can I call a friend to find out what to do? Do I need help from my Mom or Dad? What do I need help with?" and various other permutations, depending upon the task at hand. She was encouraged to keep a written list of these "inside questions" and to refer to it as and when she needed, adding to it as required. Kelly was also encouraged to talk aloud as she worked so that she could pick up her errors more easily, and also so that those working with her could understand how she was thinking and working. Her parents were advised to model this behavior as they went about their daily routines, preparing meals, fix-ing things, getting ready to go out, driving the car, and so on. Kelly's mother was a natural—she had always thought she was slightly nuts because she tended to find herself thinking out loud—but her father needed a little practice. He was embarrassed at first and it never really came naturally, but he tried his best, and was able to make some progress.

For her part, Kelly's job was obviously to do her work by herself and to avail her-self of her parents' help within the conditions that they had set. This was quite a new concept for her, and she was very reluctant at first. However, she soon found that, provided she put in a reasonable effort for the hour, she was permitted to have some leisure time, since all her privileges were reinstated and the only way that she would miss out on her TV or her telephone time was to choose to dilly-dally and procrastinate around her homework. This arrangement suited her fine. Initially, she had a very difficult time articulating what she needed help with and she needed some teaching around this issue. But the teaching didn't last long and she soon caught on to what was meant. She had the most difficulty with the concept that her homework would be taken back to school as she had done it, to be evaluated by her teachers. She was very used to presenting them with an almost-perfect, finished product, and her anxieties rocketed when she realized that it was up to her to correct her own work. Recognizing her high anxiety levels, her parents backed out of this aspect gradually, first running an eye over the work to look for glaring errors and simply underlining them in pencil, or noting the mistake in the margin. This enabled Kelly to self-correct, and even though she didn't like having made mistakes, at least she felt good about having the opportunity to put them right. The next step was for her parents to encourage her to look for her own errors. She did NOT like doing this. She figured that she had already done the work once; why should she have to go over it again? Although it took some time, she eventually decided that it was sometimes better for her to find the mistakes than for the teacher to find them, so she became a little more used to the idea that this was her choice. She could get a better mark if she chose to take the time.

Not surprisingly, the people who had the hardest time with this whole process were Kelly's parents, especially her father. It was so important to him that she succeed that he had invested a whole part of himself in her school work. Her mother was quite happy to set the timer and get on with her life, although she tended to rescue Kelly by helping her out with last-minute projects. Her father still tended to nag and threaten, and he was so deathly afraid of her failing a grade that he found it exceedingly hard to let her do her work on her own. However, he did notice that Kelly seemed proud when she managed to complete tasks by herself, and this helped him to back off a little. Neither parent was likely to let go completely for another few years—and probably neither would you or I—but at least they were able to move along the continuum, to the "prompting" and "supporting" levels, which was a great improvement in independence for Kelly. While her marks did not improve a whole lot, her teachers were more satisfied that it was Kelly's own work and they were not as nervous about recommending a continuation to high school.

For her part, Kelly learned that she could manage without her parents as crutches; she could see the relationship between her input and her output; and she began to own her own work, mistakes as well as successes. She also learned what feeling proud of yourself felt like. Most importantly, she began to learn to make good choices because there was no one in the way preventing the natural consequences of her choices from happening. If she chose to put in effort, it paid off. If she chose to ignore her mistakes, her marks dropped. If she chose to "forget" an assignment, she had to forfeit some leisure time to complete it. If she chose to study for a test, she did better than if she chose not to study. These choices all lead to ownership, responsibility and accountability—the cornerstones of independence, for life.

Letting Go

By the time our emerging-adult children approach the end of adolescence, we are experiencing several changes in our relationship with our offspring. Most importantly, we recognize that we no longer have the same degree of influence or control that we had when they were young. There is frequently precious little that we can do to motivate or stop them once they have made up their mind to do or not to do something. They are often bigger, stronger, smarter or just plain more stubborn than we are. They respond to any suggestion that they go to their room with a roll of the eyeballs and a "yeah, right!" and carry on with whatever they were doing. Short of locking them in the basement in a strait-jacket and throwing away the key, we can no longer enforce a grounding, and unless we can think of something really BIG—like the car keys or huge sums of money—we can no longer bribe with anything sufficiently attractive to compel compliance. We make noises about their "using this house like a hotel"; we resent their selfishness; we sometimes rant and rave and threaten, but somehow we are not effective in making changes. They have, in fact, become more like our roommates than our children, and our old ways are no longer working.

At this point on the road to our children's independence, there are some basic rules of thumb. They are very similar to the way in which we conduct ourselves when we deal with people in other areas of our lives, especially when those other adults are people whom we love and respect, and from whom we tolerate no abuse.

We can make requests and rely on common courtesy. While we may still occasionally get away with commands (and thus we hang on to the idea that they continue to work), there is often little we can do to enforce them and we are not doing much to enhance our adult relationship with our children. We can, however, request such things as: "I wonder if you'd mind moving your books off the dining room table so that I can set it for supper?" or "Please could you smoke outside. We are a non-smoking household." If people do not comply with our first request, we can restate it, perhaps a little more clearly, and give them a way of complying the second time without admitting any fault for noncompliance the first time around. "I guess that there's been a misunderstanding about the use of the car. I thought we had agreed that you'd have it back by midnight. Please can you make sure that you get it home on time tonight? Thanks a lot." We can also make general statements, rather than focusing on who committed a particular crime. "Someone left the dog outside in the rain. Please can everyone make sure he's in before leaving?" "There was no gas in the car when I went to use it today. Please could you make sure you fill it up next time you take it out?" "The garbage is still sitting on the back steps. I can't remember whose turn it was to take it out." Even when we are grown up, we still like to receive approval, especially from parents, and especially if we can get it without losing face.

Complying with another's request is common courtesy and good manners—and relies on mutual respect. We generally expect such compliance, even from strangers, if we ask in an appropriate way. "Excuse me, please, I wonder if you'd mind moving your shopping cart over a little? Thanks." "I wonder if you could please pass me one of those brochures." Even though we occasionally run into your standard neighborhood boor, this approach usually works well with people we do not know. However, this is a tricky one within a family if we did not build up any mutual respect while our children were young. We have to have respect for ourselves and trust in our own judgment if we expect our children to trust and respect us. We also have to let our children earn our trust and respect as they develop. These are topics for whole books all by themselves. For example, Barbara Coloroso's *Kids Are Worth It!* has this as an underlying premise in terms of "do unto others as you would have them do unto you." Suffice it to say that with trust and mutual respect in any relationship, our needs and wants are more likely to be expressed and met, and we are likely to have strong bonds to the individuals with whom we share such communication. Learning to say "I need your help with this" or "I need you to take over for a few minutes" or "I should like you to…" can be extraordinarily effective in such an environment, as can a simple "please" and "thank you."

We can give advice. Giving advice seems to be an intrinsic part of the parental job description from birth to the grave! In the good old days, and in some cultures to this day, the advice and wisdom of the older generations were sought after and treasured. These days, advice is often greeted with eye rolls, sighs and reluctant lip service. This may be because the media and Madison Avenue have done a pretty good job convincing the young that you are old at 25 and virtually dead by 30 and anything after that is not worth noticing. It also may be because we, as adults, are not very good at giving advice without it sounding like a command. We frequently do not notice that there is a difference. So when we say to a 17-year-old: "It's cold outside, I think you should wear your jacket," there is frequently an implied "… or else!" which makes it sound as if we are giving an order. Since our children tend to be quite used to us giving orders and since they expect the "… or else!" they are not very good at recognizing that this is a piece of advice that can be taken or left. They are, therefore, frequently incensed that we would continue to order them around when they consider themselves to be adults and quite capable of deciding how to dress themselves. We, on the other hand, get very upset, insulted and offended when they do not take our advice, and the "… or else!" materializes as a guilt trip, a sulk or a personal affront. Sometimes the discussion can even escalate into a consequence that was never intended: "… or else I won't let you have the car!". Advice given many times equals nagging. Advice not acknowledged encourages nagging. One of the most difficult parts of parenting—perhaps even impossible for some of us some of the time—is to continue to support our children when they refuse to take our advice. They will sometimes suffer because of this and can then learn from their mistakes. They will sometimes be dead right. Either way, they can use our support.

We can let the natural consequences of our children's actions happen. This is probably one of the hardest parts of letting go and yet one of the most critical. If our children are to survive out there, alone in the world, they will be subject to the natural consequences of their own choices and decisions. These may include: failing courses, passing courses, getting jobs, losing jobs, making friends, losing friends, causing accidents, preventing disasters, making other people angry, pleasing other people, being happy, being hurt, making money, spending money—and eventually they will get the picture. Many parents subscribe to the notion of natural consequences very early on in their child-rearing years. These are the parents and children who benefit the most. However, permitting natural consequences when our children are young may well place them in danger. For example, no one wishes to contemplate the natural consequences of allowing a child to cross a busy highway to learn that this is not a wise thing to do. In like manner, babies are not usually allowed to stick their fingers in electrical sockets to find out that this can kill them. Our son's very first word was "smack?" since this was what he was told would happen to his hand (accompanied by a realistic self-demonstration) if he pursued this less-than-safe exploration of his environment. This worked much better than a lecture about the resistance of the human body when interrupting the ampere flow of the electrical circuits in a residential setting. "Smack" he understood. It worked and we never actually had to do it, because he always made the better choice.

A good definition of maturity is the stage at which we accept the consequences of our own actions. Thus, when our children reach independence, they are in fact taking over the responsibility for their own behavior. We may have to let them run into the law if they speed, steal or smoke up. We may have to let them pay off the damage they caused out of the money earned in their minimum-wage, part-time jobs. We may decide that they must move out, if they are unwilling to make the kinds of choices consistent with the value systems of the family. In short, we may have to let them grow up. The more we rescue them and save them from learning what the consequences of their actions are, and, especially, from feeling the discomfort that these consequences bring, the longer they will take to reach maturity.

We can keep control of our own resources. Much to every teenager's surprise, there is no commandment in the Parents' Rule Book that says that we MUST: lend the car, give a reason for not lending the car, spend money on things of which we do not approve, give a reason for not spending our money on said things, pick someone up on demand or drive anyone and anyone's friends anywhere, spend time or effort on anything at all for someone who cannot even be civil, or put up with any kind of abuse even if the individual says that everyone uses that kind of language. There are few adolescents in the entire civilized world who have not heard: "This is *our* house and these are *our* rules." I do not believe that there is a single one who does not become enraged at this statement of fact!

To protect our own belongings, space, time, effort and money, we have to have some integrity and some notion of ourselves as separate, whole human beings with boundaries of our own. We have to believe that we have some self-worth and some sense of self-respect. We also have to have a firm belief that our children do not develop independence by our continuing to provide for their every activity. We have to have sufficient backbone to resist the temptation to give in and to rescue them at the first whiff of discomfort, as well as to brace for the onslaughts of our children's wrath and our own guilt when we stand firm. If our children do not budget their money adequately, they will be left short. They will feel uncomfortable or they may have to go without. They will then learn to budget their money more adequately the next time. If we fork over an advance, a loan or some extra cash (even if these are accompanied by Lecture No. 42 on Managing Your Finances), they will not feel uncomfortable and they will not have to go without. They will then learn to come to us for money. Our choice to give or to withhold money has a direct impact on the lessons our children will learn. They call it control. We call it standing up for our values.

Our grown-up children frequently spend money, time and/or effort on undertakings of which we simply do not approve. They do drugs. They smoke. They gamble. They eat endless quantities of expensive junk even though the fridge at home is full of good food. If they are old enough to do any of these things, they are old enough to pay for them out of money they earn. We do not have to be the source of that money. If they do not have an alternative source of money, they will have the choice of either giving up their various habits or finding an alternative source of money. If that alternative source of money is illegal, we are back to the subject of natural consequences. If they are angry with us for not supporting their habits, so be it. That's life. Our grown-up children have to learn that sometimes their parents disapprove of their lifestyle choices. Parents have to learn that sometimes they will disapprove of ways in which their grown-up children behave. This is also life.

The main issue is that we, as parents, also have choices. "I *have* to drive him" or "I *have* to give him money for cafeteria lunches." Actually, no you don't. Whenever we find ourselves saying "I have to…" or "I should…" we can change that to "I choose to…" and regain our sense of self and our sense of integrity—even if we are saying "I choose to be a doormat" or "I choose to subject myself entirely to my child's every whim." In this way, we can regain control of our lives and provide a superb model for our children in terms of assertiveness, self-worth and self-esteem.

A Time and a Place

One of the most common questions from parents relates to *when* to let go, when to allow children to taste the freedoms that autonomy brings. "At what age can we let our child stay alone?" "How old should a child be before you give him an allowance?" "How do I know if my child is old enough to walk to school unaccompanied?" There is no simple answer. There is no magic age. Some children are born responsible; others never get there. One 11-year-old may be able to stay alone in the house; another 14-year-old may not. This is where it can be helpful to keep in mind that there is absolutely no rule that says we must treat all of our children equally, nor that reaching a particular age is an automatic ticket to freedom.

Most parents know their children well enough to know when they are ready for a little more responsibility or for a loosening of the reins. However, many of us take a huge leap from *doing* or *directing* straight to letting go, forgetting that there are a number of other steps in between. This may be too much for our children and they may fail miserably at their first try. It may be too much for us and we may have to pull back and take a smaller step the next time.

It can be helpful to do a check on where we are on the continuum of letting each of our children go in each of the main areas of their lives. The following table provides some sample behaviors that we would eventually expect our children to "own," without our involvement. For young children, we should expect a high degree of parental involvement; for teens, far less, perhaps even none. This is not a magazine questionnaire where a certain number of points means you've won! It is simply a means for a self-check to see where we and our children are on a few aspects of independence, and to give us an idea of what the next step might be. Do we still have some skills to teach in any specific areas? Are we stuck at doing or directing? Does our child know exactly what to do but is allowing us to do things for him? Are we letting go before our children have learned the skills they require to survive in the world outside the family? We can look at our own individual profile with each child separately, and see.

Areas of Independence	My Current Involvement						
	do 0	direct 1	teach 2	help 3	prompt 4	support 5	let go 6

Self-help:

personal hygiene	0	1	2	3	4	5	6
meal preparation	0	1	2	3	4	5	6
handling money	0	1	2	3	4	5	6

Social:

sharing	0	1	2	3	4	5	6
holding a conversation	0	1	2	3	4	5	6
politeness/manners	0	1	2	3	4	5	6
conflict resolution	0	1	2	3	4	5	6
managing "down" time	0	1	2	3	4	5	6
taking turns	0	1	2	3	4	5	6
making/maintaining friendships	0	1	2	3	4	5	6

Learning:

listening to others	0	1	2	3	4	5	6
task completion (start to finish)	0	1	2	3	4	5	6
following instructions	0	1	2	3	4	5	6
working alone	0	1	2	3	4	5	6
homework	0	1	2	3	4	5	6
task breakdown into steps	0	1	2	3	4	5	6
initiating learning activities	0	1	2	3	4	5	6

Values:

spiritual (e.g., going to church)	0	1	2	3	4	5	6
establishing own morals	0	1	2	3	4	5	6
lifestyle choices	0	1	2	3	4	5	6
relationships	0	1	2	3	4	5	6
care of the environment	0	1	2	3	4	5	6

Health:

nutrition	0	1	2	3	4	5	6
exercise	0	1	2	3	4	5	6
bedtime/sleep	0	1	2	3	4	5	6
care of own environment	0	1	2	3	4	5	6
habits: alcohol/ nicotine/other drugs	0	1	2	3	4	5	6
sexuality	0	1	2	3	4	5	6

Safety:

"rules of the road"	0	1	2	3	4	5	6
street proofing	0	1	2	3	4	5	6
using appliances	0	1	2	3	4	5	6
setting curfews	0	1	2	3	4	5	6
self-defence	0	1	2	3	4	5	6
using public transportation	0	1	2	3	4	5	6
safe sex practices	0	1	2	3	4	5	6
use of medication/drugs	0	1	2	3	4	5	6
defensive driving	0	1	2	3	4	5	6

Easier Said Than Done

The separation of parent and child is a natural process, meant to happen at some point toward the end of adolescence. In the majority of families, children leave home when they go away to school, move in with friends or get married. Some leave to travel the world and some leave simply to gain their independence. This event may bring ambivalence at best and pain at worst. In families where there has been no gradual movement toward the inevitable exit from the nest, there may be abrupt, sometimes even quite brutal, action to sever the ties. Some children, who have been abused at home, leave not only suddenly but early, frequently well before they are prepared to tackle a normal world where trust and consideration are major keys to relationships. But they quit to survive. Some leave because they hear about the Wonderful World of Welfare, where teenagers are given more money than they have ever held in their hand at any one time, where there are no rules, and where they can buy their freedom. They may even choose to live on the streets.

For many teens, the course of adolescence has run more smoothly and there has been a normal tendency for them to spend gradually increasing amounts of time away from parents and siblings. They may be involved in sports or arts activities or other hobbies that take up many hours; they will almost certainly have spent hour after hour with friends, in person or on the phone. They may be holding down a part-time job. They may even do homework. They may shut themselves in their rooms for hours at a time and emerge only to empty the fridge. Their biological clocks may be ticking somewhat out of sync with the rest of the family's, with sleep patterns changing and mealtimes becoming somewhat erratic. By the time they reach their last year of high school, they may be out of the house more than they are in and have probably spent prolonged periods away with friends or staying at home while the rest of the family travels. Many of them are autonomous with respect to transportation and meal preparation (or at least meal consumption). Sometimes, they are approaching financial independence, budgeting their own money, contributing toward room and board, saving for post-secondary education and even making some significant purchases of their own.

Still others have been somewhat indulged and sheltered from the realities of the real world outside the family. They have been given most of what they have asked for—sometimes accompanied by some grumbling on the part of their generous parents, but given nonetheless. At some level, they believe that money grows on trees, or at least can be acquired simply by feeding a plastic card into a bank machine. In some cases, they have been repeatedly *told* about money: that they need to earn some; that the pit is not bottomless; that if they are not careful with their things they will not be given any more; that they need to learn its value; that they cannot treat home like a hotel, and so forth. However, they have not been permitted to experience the discomfort that comes with running out of money, of actually having none left, and having to do without whatever it is they want until they can afford to pay for it. They often have not had to pay back "loans" and they have simply expected their coffers to be topped up whenever they run low. Somewhat like "lifers" in an institution, they have had free room, board, clothing, leisure, education and transportation for as long as they can remember and they are ill-equipped for life on the outside. They know this and we know this. As parents who have chosen this route, we also are ill-equipped to let our children go. Frequently, one of us has been a full-time parent who has made it his or her life's work to cater to our children's every want and need, or we may have tried to assuage our guilt at being a working family by making sure our children's demands are met. When they leave us, we also see part of ourselves go. We realize that they cannot manage. Sometimes, we try to prevent them leaving by telling them that if they go, they are gone for good. This makes them even more nervous about leaving and, sometimes, very hard for them to come back, if they cannot or do not cope. They sometimes quit before they are fired. We sometimes fire them before they can quit. Often, individuals need to climb down from high horses with some degree of grace; in other words, to find a way out of the conflict without losing face. It is frequently the 20-20 vision of hindsight that shows us we had some other options.

However, even when our children have been well-prepared for their independence, the actual wrench of letting go can be quite traumatic for us or them. As in any circumstances where the anxiety levels run high, anger may be the surface emotion splattered all over the walls. We may find ourselves fighting over small, insignificant issues as our children pack. It is frequently easier to leave someone when we are angry than when we are loving and sad. Children who travel back and forth between separated or divorced parents experience this roller coaster every time they change homes. Being aware that this is due to sadness or anxiety, rather than to defiance or obstreperousness, can make handling the situation much easier for everyone. Children leaving for university can be equally anxious or sad. They may be apprehensive about what the future holds, about making new friends or leaving old ones, about the pressures they will face and the competitive world they are about to enter. They may not realize for some weeks how homesick they are and what they miss about the daily hassles of life in the family. Away from home for the first time, they experience the loneliness of having no one to take for granted, and they often fall sick with no one to take care of them. Most of us had parents who told us that we wouldn't appreciate them until we left home. They were right.

In addition to the way our children are feeling, we ourselves may be surprised at the waves of depression that wash over us as our nest empties.

Somehow the time has gone so fast. The sight of our son in his prom-night finery brought back intense memories of his one time as a ring bearer at his uncle's wedding when he was four years old (or was it yesterday?), dressed in his gray tuxedo and bow tie, walking down the aisle next to a pretty little girl who resembled a pink lampshade. Fair brought a tear to the old eye, I can tell you. I bawled all the way home from depositing our firstborn *and* our middle child *and* our 6' 2" baby in their residence cells—connecting with a deep sense of loss mingled with relief and pride. My husband's eyes were not totally dry, either. He has mourned the loss of his children's child-hoods deeply, but has welcomed them back as adult companions with a renewed sense of hope for the future. We have done most of what we can, despite a nagging sense that it is not enough, and an overwhelming urge to do more. They can stand alone.

Hanging On

There is no question that, at some level, we NEVER let go. It doesn't mat-ter how old or sophisticated or independent our children become. In partic-ular, that old instinct to protect keeps us hanging on to the notion that we are somehow responsible for keeping them safe for ever. It was a credit to the tenacity of my Mom's maternal instinct the very last time we saw each other, in the hospital, her body wasted and wracked with toxic chemicals and the dreadful disease they were trying to subdue. She grabbed my hand one last time, looked at me with her full attention as I left to catch the plane that was to take me back to my husband and children, half a world away in distance and an infinity in time, and whispered: "Mind how you go!"

When our teenagers are pushing the limits of independence, we tend to stuff as much as we possibly can into the definition of "safety issue" to jus-tify our continued interventions and control. While knowing that they will under no circumstances drive when they have been drinking is clearly a safety issue, and knowing roughly where they are and when they will be home are certainly closely related, knowing the telephone numbers of all their friends is not. Neither is reading their diaries or searching their rooms without their knowledge, although many parents would argue differently. We lose credibility when we overstuff this particular sack. Then our children may no longer trust our genuine and necessary concern.

The difficulties that we, as parents, have in comprehending that our children are eventually able to keep themselves safe became evident in our family just a few months ago. Our older daughter and her boyfriend were driving from Hamilton to Boston for a few days and she was planning to drive back alone. She has lived away from home, quite independently and happily, including a stint overseas, for almost seven years. She is a totally competent young lady, fully fit, trained in various aspects of emergency medicine, quite capable of taking care of herself in most of the dire circumstances I can envisage. Nonetheless, before she started on her journey, my husband and I found ourselves on the telephone, one on each extension, in the following unidirectional "conversation."

Me: "Now, remember, Boston is not a safe place. Don't *ever* go out alone. Stay in the main areas where there are lots of people and stay away from the back streets. Cross the street if you see gangs of people hanging around. Don't wear your gold chain in case a mugger rips it off. Make sure you always have some identification on you and carry our names and address somewhere in your wallet. Don't carry much money with you. If you are mugged, don't resist. Keep your cell phone with you at all times. Call us when you get there and let us know the address where you'll be staying."

Her Dad: "Make sure you've checked the car and that it has oil and a full tank of gas before you leave. Check that the windshield wipers are working and that you have enough washer fluid. Make sure the spare tire is pumped up. If the muffler falls off, use the duct tape I gave you and it'll be fine until you get home. Stay on the freeways and make sure you have money for the tolls. On the way back, make sure that you stop every couple of hours, get out and have a walk or a jog for a few minutes. If you feel at all tired, PULL OVER and grab some sleep. If you break down, lock your doors and use your cell phone. Don't open the door to anyone unless they show you some identification."

Both of us: "Have fun!"

We could HEAR her rolling her eyes.

Chapter 13

Three Big Goals of Parenting

Throughout this book, we have essentially looked at a wide range of parenting goals aimed at raising independent, happy children and adults. It is next to impossible to try to place these goals in any kind of rank order, since at various times, in various situations and with various children, each one could legitimately be more pressing than the others. However, in my experience with both parents *and* teachers, three goals remain head and shoulders above the others in terms of their relevance to the overall, long-term process of raising truly healthy human beings.

© Lynn Johnston Productions Inc./Distributed by United Feature Syndicate, Inc. Reprinted with permission.

Goal #3
Loving them enough to set limits

Why do we need to set limits on our children at all? Why is simply loving them and letting them discover their own limits not enough? Wouldn't it be easier? Wouldn't they just discover for themselves how to be happy, well-adjusted adults?

Would it be easier? Probably. Would they discover how to be compassionate, thoughtful, empathic, considerate, polite, respectful and—through these—ultimately happy? Probably not. We are not *born* with any of these characteristics. Human beings are, by nature, born full of self-serving drives, to satisfy basic, primal urges, such as hunger, thirst, sex, survival. We are innately equipped with a fight-or-flight reaction to stress and we have a strong inclination to save ourselves before we save others.

Initially, parent and child are one. Limits help children understand where they end and we begin. In other words, limits help them to differentiate themselves from others and to develop a sense of "self" that exists separate from the world around them. Within these limits, children are free to develop the independent characteristics that will help them to define their own parameters as adults. Without limits, in extreme cases, children may develop into adults with what are known as borderline personality characteristics—where they lack a clearly defined sense of "ego," which is the balance between the primal, inborn drives and the progressively internalized policing function, served initially by parents and other authority figures, and eventually by self-discipline and self-control.

Thus, if we are to encourage each successive generation to acquire the altruistic, prosocial skills required to function in what we see as a civilized society, we have to *turn* our children into separate individuals with a conscience. As their parents and teachers, we have to *make* them write thank you notes, return things they borrow or steal, fix things they break, tell the truth, try things on their own, take turns and share, care for others' feelings, accept responsibility for their actions, go to church or mosque or synagogue or temple, behave kindly toward people and animals, and—when appropriate—be capable of putting others' needs before their own. If we fail to achieve this goal by example and encouragement alone, our only option is to decide what they need to do and to demand that they do it. We do this by defining what we expect and supporting them in their attempts to achieve these expectations. As responsible adults, we must ensure that our expectations are reasonable and that they fit the general norms of social acceptability, and we must be flexible to account for individual differences, environmental constraints and situational demands. We do all this because we love them enough to realize that being an outcast in society ultimately threatens survival.

In the fields of child development and child psychology in general, it has long been known that one particular style of parenting produces the "best-adjusted" children; these children are well-behaved, compassionate and caring, respectful of authority and very self-aware. The style of parenting is known as AUTHORITATIVE. Authoritative parents are warm and accepting of their children, raising them in a nurturing atmosphere, in which individual differences are recognized and differential needs are understood. In addition, authoritative parents provide structure and guidance to the children in the family. They set boundaries on behavior and uphold these boundaries in a kind but firm way. They choose the limits in accordance with the child's developmental level and competencies, and ensure that the child is in possession of the necessary skills before they expect to delegate each particular responsibility. They pick their fights carefully and do not sweat the small stuff. They let children set their own limits as soon as they show that they are ready. Authoritative parents are also human. They do not always do all these things with good grace. They make mistakes. They put out fires. They excel in damage control. They occasionally freak. But they do not stray from their two basic beliefs: that children need unconditional acceptance for who they are, and that the world is a safer place when children can trust the limits set by the significant adults in their young lives.

Many people completely misunderstand the notion of *authoritative* parenting. They confuse *authoritative* with *authoritarian* and start to get hot under the collar about returning to Victorian, child-rearing techniques when limits were rigid, punishment was the order of the day, and children were definitely seen and not heard. The *authoritarian* adult indeed believes in changing the child's behavior by means of power alone and does not entertain the notion of reason. Children are kept at a distance at best, rejected completely at worst, and the atmosphere is cool and not particularly conducive to warm family relationships. Love is lacking. The children of authoritarian parents tend to be withdrawn and sullen, quarrelsome and inhibited, and sometimes even depressed. Most of us recognize that, given a choice, it is not good for either us or our children to adopt this parenting style as a preference.

The provision of structure and guidance for children is in a completely different dimension from coldness, rejection and the wielding of adult power. If we refuse to set limits for children because we are afraid that we will become cruel, rigid and hard, and that our children will reject us, we are, in fact, denying them the opportunity to learn to trust us, and, from that trust, to be able to form other lasting bonds and relationships with a diverse set of people (and animals!) for the rest of their lives. Limits are the stepping stones in the quicksand of life and show children where they are safe. There is no question that, as they grow up, they will test these same limits and start to provide alternative stepping stones for themselves.

Yet others feel that, to show warmth, acceptance and love, they should be *permissive* and allow children a free rein in whatever they wish to do. This is, at least in part, because our children (and sometimes other adults) spend much time trying to convince us that "if you loved me, you'd let me" do all kinds of things. *Permissive* parents do not believe in setting limits, or, on the other hand, may set all kinds of limits in theory but not uphold them in practice. Allowing children to do as they please is frequently seen as a quick and easy means of keeping them happy. It is reinforced almost immediately, because it probably works. In the short term, at least. We have a very hard time saying "no" to our children and we believe that, if our children are happy, we must be good parents. While children of permissive parents are frequently quite independent, creative and have high levels of initiative—all characteristics that we like to see in our offspring—the dangers arise when *permissive* becomes *passive*, our children's independence, creativity and initiative start to get out of hand, and we lose the ability to intervene effectively when required. Since our children have not learned to respect legitimate authority because we have not taught them how, other adults may also have great difficulty imposing limits and providing guidance. Children of permissive parents tend to ignore authority, may be rebellious or disobedient, and lack the necessary boundaries that allow them to function successfully in society at large.

Each of our children is unique and elicits from each parent a different set of responses. One child may stick out his chin in defiance in the face of utterly inevitable disaster, while another may crumble at the raising of an eyebrow. One baby may become still and calm when held; another may become frantic. We may have a preferred parenting style. We may prefer to be authoritative when the circumstances are right and the children are cooperative. We may be able to be authoritative when the children are being compliant. However, we may have a bad-hair day or come home in a grumpy mood to find the children being overly creative with the cat, or we may be genuinely preoccupied with higher priority issues, such as a death in the family or a major life crisis. On such a day, or sometimes even with one particular child whose voice strikes the frequency that causes the hairs on the back of our neck to resonate, we may well become quite authoritarian, even though this would normally go against the grain. On a day when we are perhaps feeling burned out or overburdened, or when we simply cannot be bothered to think up or uphold consequences for our children's choices, we may abandon the rules and let the children do as they please. We may, for a time at least, become permissive.

What is surprising to some is that our children's behavior will change accordingly. When we are permissive, they will behave like the children of permissive parents. When we are authoritarian, they will behave like the children of authoritarian parents. And when we can become authoritative again, they will be well-adjusted once again.

The other side of the same coin is that, given that parenting is a two-way street, our children's behavior at any given time will strongly influence our parenting behavior. Children who are behaving in a delinquent, acting-out fashion may cause our style to change from being permissive to imposing more rules in an attempt to bring order out of chaos. Thus, depending on whether we feel cool and preoccupied, or warm and fuzzy, we become either authoritarian or authoritative—and our children's behavior changes again. It becomes clear that the direction of this change depends primarily upon whether we treat them with some warmth and nurturing, or whether we keep them at a distance.

If we truly love our children, we want them to be well-adjusted adults who know how to set limits for themselves to live comfortably in whatever social world they eventually choose for themselves. In addition to providing them with clear boundaries and support, we need to demonstrate self-discipline and self-control, and encourage them to set their own limits, by which to run their own lives. At that time, they will be able to separate themselves appropriately, confidently and completely from us. Allowing them to do so is the ultimate act of love as a parent.

Goal #2
Giving ourselves permission to parent

To accomplish the tasks of parenting, we must give ourselves permission to be leaders in the family group. We must be willing to take charge, to plan long-term goals and to make decisions, even if they are unpopular.

In generations past, this was never an issue. Parents had clear roles: the males were the sole breadwinners; the females stayed at home to tend the house and raise the children. It was not until the early part of the 20th century that children were even seen to exist as anything but small adults, even in eras when a frighteningly short life expectancy made what we now call "adolescence" in fact "middle age." The growth of the "child" as a legitimate section of society proceeded slowly throughout the early part of the century, but came to the fore in the late '40s and early '50s with the evolution of the baby boomers. These children were highly valued as the pioneers of a new age following the devastation of World War II and their sheer numbers have made them a sociological *tsunami*. They have swept aside traditional roles and expectations and forged pathways for themselves and the generations that follow. They followed the footsteps of their mothers and grandmothers on the path toward the liberation of women from their traditional roles and made an industry out of parenting. As the baby boomers grew up, advertisers discovered the buying potential of parents who yearned to give their children whatever they wanted and whose children wanted whatever they saw. The combination of this discovery and the explosion of the mass media resulted in children being essential to the survival of billions of dollars-worth of business in the so-called New World. The ability of the media to expose such societal evils as child abuse and neglect should have been positive in encouraging society to eliminate them. What has transpired, however, is some confusion between the type and degree of rigidity and expectations that are totally unrealistic or abusive, and the genuine need for adults to be in control of children who cannot function independently. As a result, parents have become increasingly afraid to discipline their children, since "discipline" has moved from its root meaning of "teaching" to take on the inferences of punishment, suppression and oppression, and has taken on the air of a four-letter word.

At the same time, educators were inventing child-centered, discovery learning. From Jean Piaget to Maria Montessori and Benjamin Spock, experts were espousing the need to expose children to a stimulating environment where they would be free to discover rather than wait to be taught. In the late '80s and in the '90s, this approach has reached epidemic proportions, to the point where, in some areas, almost everything in the classroom is child-led. Friends of ours experienced a situation where they were not allowed to see samples of their 10-year-old daughter's classroom work without her permission. Children as young as kindergarten-age "lead" parent-teacher interviews and are expected to evaluate their own work, along with that of their peers. Unfortunately, there is little evidence to indicate that this approach produces more socially responsible, educated or competent young adults. In fact, incidences of violence in schools are increasing, attacks against teachers are on the rise, the number of school drop-outs is not declining, and the vast majority of teachers and administrators will tell you that they feel powerless to make the changes that they *know* are essential to bring education back under control. This does not necessarily mean a return to sitting in rows, being swatted on the back of the hand with a wooden ruler. It does, however, mean a return to a hierarchy within the system, with the main power in the hands of those who have the wisdom and ability to use it well.

Throughout much of our adult lives, we rely on the sagacity of our leaders to make major decisions. Luckily, in our democratic society, we have the opportunity to vote for many of these individuals and the responsibility to exercise this franchise. The power of the press moguls and the pollsters to manipulate public opinion is a topic for another day. Suffice it to say, that we frequently have no option but to go along with decisions that are made for us and cast in the stone of legislation. We must pay taxes; we must adhere to the laws of the land; we must drive on a given side of the street, and so on. Most such decisions are made, supposedly, in the interests of the majority while protecting the rights of the minorities. When our own or our family's best interests do not seem to be served in this so-called democratic process, we begin to feel anxious and insecure. We realize how unnerving it can be to lose faith in the political leaders in whose hands we placed our trust.

Consider, in addition, any situation in which we rely on another individual's expertise. How do we feel when we come to the realization, either suddenly or over time, that he or she does not know the answer? In our family, for example, I rely extensively on my husband's judgment on wilderness camping trips. Born and raised in the middle of a big city, I have always found myself adrift when my immediate environment does not include a telephone and a nearby hospital. Blessed with a vivid imagination and a well-honed capacity for foreseeing disaster, I panic with consummate ease in the wilderness where each sound could herald the imminent arrival of a grizzly bear, where each swing of the ax or slice of the knife could potentially sever a digit or a limb, and where each bend of the river could hurtle a canoe over waterfalls of cartoon-like proportion and land us in the middle of who-knows-where. I rely totally on the look of calm in my husband's eyes and the raising of an eyebrow to question my very sanity in even suggesting that there might be the hint of anything remotely worth worrying about. Imagine, then, my horror when—in response to my hysterical cry of "But isn't that *dangerous*?" or "*Shouldn't we be there by now?*"—he furrows his usually unfurrowable brow, and says "Hmmmm" in a dubious tone that at once tells me we are doomed to a slow horrible death; we will be eaten alive by some wild animals or mosquitoes, or else we are hopelessly lost and will never see civilization again. At that point, I legitimately freak.

The point here is simply that children need to rely on adults they can trust to learn to explore the world by themselves. We must be those adults. We must, as parents and teachers, take the responsibility for making decisions that are for the good of the individuals in the group. This is effortless as long as the decisions are popular. In fact, we usually try for consensus, even if we have to work hard at it, and much of the time we succeed. Getting children to comply is easy when they agree. Having them adhere to a rule or expectation is simple when the reason for doing so is clear and/or when we can persuade them to agree with the reason.

The tough part of parenting is being a leader under difficult circumstances; when we do not want to be a leader; when we feel we lack the qualifications for the job. Inside most of us is the little child that just wants to be looked after—some of us more than others—and it is almost impossible to take charge when this child's needs are crying out to be met. Even those of us who are confident and comfortable with leadership have days when we desperately want someone else to make a decision or take over our responsibilities. I have met many highly competent individuals, a majority of them women, who are burned out being "strong" and who yearn for someone else to take the reins for a while.

Small group research has shown that, when a leader is not appointed, one will emerge. The problem in a family is that that "leader" may be a young child or a teenager—if the adults in the group have abdicated from the job. Children do not have the knowledge, skills or experience to lead a family. If they find themselves taking over the job—by default in the case of parents who have abdicated due to inadequate levels of motivation or energy for the job, or by design in the case of parents who believe that they are oppressing children by insisting on adult leadership—they are almost universally anxious. Such anxiety, especially in the face of abandonment by parent figures, leads either to depression in children who internalize their feelings or to aggression in those children who externalize. Children-in-Charge are almost always unhappy.

Health and mental-health professionals, by and large, have been instrumental in exacerbating a situation where parents have lost confidence in their own abilities to parent. Many parents have been persuaded that there are other people "out there" who know how to look after our children much better than we do. These people know, among many other things, how to talk so kids will listen, raise the spirited child, cope with attention-deficit disorder, increase their child's intelligence, toilet-train in 24 hours, provide quality child care, guarantee a superb educational milieu, and ensure that children never, ever get sick because they are fed exactly the right nutrients in exactly the correct proportions. Excuse us if we come to believe that we are inadequate, if not totally incompetent. We need to learn to use these people as consultants, if and when we need them, rather than as gurus who could be much better parents than we are.

We need to stop looking for THE plan or THE right way to do this parenting business. It simply does not exist. We need to trust our own intuition and to draft our own plan. As Virginia Satir has said, we, the parents, are the "architects" of the family. To help us with this plan, if we get one workable idea from each book we read, workshop we attend, lecture we listen to, TV program we watch, expert we consult, we are doing pretty well. We do not need to berate ourselves simply because we did not think of this idea all by ourselves; nor do we need to feel guilty if we have been doing things differently. I have yet to meet a single, individual parent who deliberately made a bad parenting decision. We simply do not stand there, with a good decision in one hand and a bad one in the other, and decide to choose the bad one. We may realize as little as a split second later that there were unforeseen consequences to that decision and we may need to make additional choices, but the point is that at the time we made a good decision, given the information we had at hand.

As parents, we have the responsibility to be as good as we can be. If we don't know how to parent, we have the obligation to find out. If we know we aren't good at it, we have the duty to improve. Even if we *are* good at it, we can still look for ways to expand our knowledge and skills. We simply cannot let our children wait years and years until we get our act together. We must do that in parallel with the job of raising them. Fair? Maybe not. Easy? Definitely not. But absolutely necessary.

We also have the right to pat ourselves on the back when we see ourselves doing well. We must be able to take pride in our work and to see the small steps that signify that what we are doing is making a difference. We can see this in the struggles of the two-year-old and his "MY do it!"; in the defiance of the five-year-old testing the limits of what she eats and when she has to follow the rules; in the very first time we realize that our child is shaped by influences other than our own and that this is not entirely a bad thing; in the rebellion of the young adolescent, who has realized his power to shut out his parents and to be a different person than the one they want him to be; in the ambivalence of the high-school graduate as she finally gets what she wished for, her ticket out of home. It is when we see our children grow into competent adults and move on that we realize that we have completed our mission, and that their every step towards independence is a triumph for them and for us.

Goal #1
Showing them that there is hope for the future

This is the principal goal of parenting. It embodies the whole notion of letting our children see that growing up and becoming an adult is not only worthwhile, it is something to which to aspire. It enables children to look forward to the future with a sense of optimism and to see themselves as instrumental in making changes and improving the world in which they and their children will live.

Our children are surrounded by doom and gloom. Doom and gloom sell papers. Doom and gloom dominate news broadcasts. The dollar goes up—the economy is falling apart. The dollar goes down—the economy is falling apart. It's a hot day—global warming. It's a cool day—it's the depleting ozone layer. They hear about all the disasters that are befalling humankind and realize that they can do nothing to stop them. They hear that marriages end in divorce and that families fall apart. They are told that the unemployment rate among young people is soaring and that there are no jobs out there. In Canada, they hear that the country is likely to fall apart—and if one does not have a country, what security does one have? In the land of plenty, they are told that they are experiencing a declining standard of living. They grow up believing that they cannot trust politicians, that even priests are abusers, and that if they don't like their parents' rules they can leave home and go on welfare.

We may tut-tut at all of this. Yet we are not helping. When is the last time you came home, walked in the door and said: "Boy! I LOVE my job! My life is SO fulfilling! I get such a wonderful buzz out of being your parent! I am SO glad we had kids!" We tend to make comments such as: "I don't know what you are complaining about. Your teen years are the best years of your life!" Of course they are not! There are few of us who would go back to the uncertainties and insecurities of adolescence, unless we could go back knowing what we know now. The teen years can be turbulent and anxiety-provoking. They can also contain some gems of moments, so we need to be realistic.

We need to know that we are major role models for our children, even though they spend the majority of their adolescence making us feel as if we are the last people they look to for advice or inspiration. If we are satisfied with our lives, it will show. If we are not, it doesn't matter what we say, our children will be watching the picture. If, as adults, we spend 24 hours a day stuck in a rut and make no attempt to change our lot in life, our children will quite likely pick up the idea that life cannot be changed.

It is our job as parents to ensure that our children receive balanced information. They need to hear from us, for example, that an unemployment rate of 15 percent in their age group may be double what it is for older people, but it still means that 85 percent of their peers are employed. They need to understand that, for the media, good news frequently does not make good headlines. We have to help them maintain a perspective, so that they realize that I am not a loser because I did not have a hit record or make the Olympics or fit into a size 4 pair of jeans. They do not need us to dwell on how they will never get a job, how they have to get marks in the 90s if they want to stand an earthly chance of being somebody, how we don't want them to turn out like their no-good friends, or how we simply can't stand their dreadful fashions, trends or music. And we cannot make up for any of these negative attitudes by patting ourselves on the back for giving them all the material goods anyone could possibly want. "But we've always given him everything! How can he *possibly* be unhappy?"

If we give our children everything, they have no need to wish and no need to dream. Wishes and dreams come from being able to want things and to work toward getting them some day—or not, as the case may be. We live in a world of instant gratification: drive-throughs, fast food, automated teller machines, computers, e-mail, fax, synchronized traffic signals, air travel.

We have little that we have to wait for. According to news reports, the average Canadian parent spends about $700 per child at Christmas. I did not believe it, until I realized that I was meeting parents who were depressed because they could not afford everything on their child's Christmas "wish list," or who were angry with their children for putting too much on the list. "Doesn't she realize that skis cost a fortune!" "But he already has a decent pair of running shoes. Why would he ask for another?" I have also met many parents who do not believe in giving their children an allowance. "Why would she want money? I buy her everything she wants!"

I have always been a dreamer. When I was a teenager, I used to dream of having the most beautiful white wedding dress in the whole world and floating down the aisle with George Harrison at my side. I dreamed of being unbelievably rich and famous. I still do! I still dream of living by the ocean or on a mountain in houses I systematically search for in magazines. I also wish. I wish for things that I really want to happen: my children always being safe and healthy; my husband never getting sick or old or infirm; my sister finding contentment in herself. Sometimes wishing and praying take on an indistinguishable quality, although I was always taught that the latter was also supposed to include some measure of gratitude and requests for forgiveness. I cannot imagine life without my wishes and my dreams.

We sometimes encounter people who feel inadequate if they cannot fulfill our wishes and our dreams. It is hard for such individuals to understand that we dreamers do not expect our wishes to be granted. What would be left? We'd probably think up more dreams, but then we would be seen as pretty tiresome and demanding, with an endless supply of needs to be met.

We should *never* confuse needs with wants or wishes or dreams. While it is a parent's job to meet a child's needs, it is simply not possible—and, I would argue, not healthy—to meet all a child's wants, wishes or dreams. Let us teach our children to hope and to look forward to reaching a longer-term goal. As such, we are providing them with a priceless gift. We are teaching them that some things are worth the wait, and that there is a greater measure of satisfaction in earning a reward by taking small steps, one at a time, than in achieving instant gratification. We are also teaching them to cope with disappointment, and to develop a broader range of strategies to attempt to reach their goals.

One of the less comfortable aspects of my day job as a psychologist is dealing with youngsters who, for whatever reason, have attempted suicide. I have long given up trying to categorize these sad individuals or to put together a list of the risk factors in their lives that would help us all, parents and professionals alike, predict which of our children are likely to reach the point where they feel they have no other way out. For each one who has nothing, there is one who has everything. For each one from a chaotic, fragmented family, there is one from a loving home. And for each one who has reflected long and hard about the decision, there is one who is impulsive. At least the fact that they are still alive offers some hope that they will choose to remain that way. One thing is for sure. They do not see any compelling reason to grow up. We can at least try to give them reasons.

A life force for many of us is to find both passion and joy. Passion may well be found in relationships, if we are lucky, but is more likely to be rooted in positive energy for life in a broad range of areas—beauty, the outdoors, dogs, cats, golf, horseback riding, ballet, cycling, skiing, the theatre, music, movies, books, the ocean—you pick. Do you have a passion? Do you find joy in everyday living? If you do, the chances are that your children do also. Not necessarily with the identical focus, but the experience of passion, nonetheless. We have to be careful not to deflate our children's passions simply because they are different from our own. We must be alert to hearing ourselves say: "I don't know why on earth you want to…" They do and that's all there is to it. Their passions may well reflect the times in which they live and we may not always understand what it is that makes them passionate. The mere fact that they can feel as deeply as we can about something that they perceive as important is meaningful in itself. Passions and dreams are frequently intertwined in the same individual, and both provide reasons for carrying on.

It goes without saying that children need parents who have a positive outlook on life, who see themselves as competent and confident, and who know the difference between the things in life that can be changed and those that cannot. It also goes without saying that many adults do not have these attributes. If we are to parent our children to the best of our abilities, we must take care of ourselves and our parenting team. We need to get a life—as individuals and as a couple—that provides us with some daily measure of satisfaction and success. We must set goals that are achievable and then take small steps to achieve them. We need to set time aside for those who matter to us—our partner, our family, our friends—so that children see that adult relationships are important and bring pleasure. We need to recognize the power of one and make the small changes within ourselves that will have an impact on our lives and those of our family, even if they will not change the world. We may do this with the help of a higher power, or with a little help from our friends, or we may do it alone from within. Our children cannot be the sole reason for our happiness, or for the success of our marital relationship, our sense of self-worth or our existence. They should not have such a huge responsibility. Neither can they wait to be parented until we get all of this sorted out. To quote Barbara Coloroso: "parenting is neither cost efficient nor time efficient." And we must never be afraid to ask for help when we need it.

We MUST give our children hope for the future. We must help them see the half of the glass that is full and encourage them to make the most of whatever they have, however much or however little. We must help them see that life is worth it. If we do not, we cannot guarantee that anyone else will.

So—love your children enough to set them limits, give yourself permission to be a parent—and get a life! Then when your children are asleep, you can creep in, sit down and look at their sleeping faces and know that you are doing the job of a lifetime, and being the best you can be. At least, until the next morning.

Epilogue

With parenting, as with most of life, the more we know, the more we realize there is to know. For some, this can be daunting and leave us feeling overwhelmed to the point of discouragement and defeat. For others, it provides infinite motivation in the quest for more knowledge. To parallel the philosophies of Scott Peck in *The Road Less Traveled,* parenting is difficult. Once we realize it is difficult, it is no longer as difficult. And who ever said it was easy? As a final word, we shall take a look at a summary of the Top Ten Goals for parents—and teachers—in reverse order, David Letterman style. Please feel free to eliminate or change those you don't agree with and add your own. It's not *what* these goals are, it's the fact that we have some that counts.

10. To enable and support our children to grow from dependence to independence.
9. To have a vision of what we want to accomplish and the courage to set policies to go with it.
8. To know our own values and to teach our children what is right and what is wrong.
7. To teach children to make good choices and to permit them to experience the consequences.
6. To ensure that parents and teachers are on the same team.
5. To watch the picture to recognize and acknowledge the small steps to success.
4. To encourage healthy communication within the family.
3. To love them enough to set reasonable limits until they can set limits of their own.
2. To give ourselves permission to be leaders in the family.
1. To show our children that there is hope for the future.

Oh, and by the way, mind how you go!

Bibliography

Bombeck, Erma: *Motherhood: The Second Oldest Profession*, G.K. Hall, Boston, Mass., 1984

Brazelton, T. Berry: *Toddlers and Parents: A Declaration of Independence* (Revised Edition), Delacorte Press/Seymour Lawrence, New York, 1989

Coloroso, Barbara: *Kids Are Worth It! Giving Your Child the Gift of Inner Discipline*, Somerville House Publishing, Toronto, Ontario, 1995

Faber, Adele and Mazlish, Elaine: *Siblings Without Rivalry*, Norton, New York, 1987

Faber, Adele and Mazlish, Elaine: *How to Talk So Kids Can Learn: At Home and In School*, Fireside Books, New York, 1996

George, Elizabeth: *Missing Joseph,* Bantam Books, New York, 1993

Johnston, Lynn: *Growing Like a Weed: For Better or For Worse Collection*, Andrews McMeel Publishing, Kansas City, 1998

Kene, Gary: *Communicate*, Volume 7, Number 11, Spring 1995

Kirkman, Rick and Scott, Jerry: *Check Please...Baby Blues 9 Scrapbook*, Andrews McMeel Publishing, Kansas City, 1998

Leach, Penelope: *Your Baby and Child from Birth to Age Five*, A. A. Knopf, New York, 1989

Mamen, Maggie: *Who's in Charge? A Guide to Family Management*, Creative Bound Inc., Carp, Ontario, 1997

Peck, M. Scott: *The Road Less Traveled: A New Psychology of Love, Traditional Values and Spiritual Growth*, Simon & Shuster, New York, 1978

Phelan, Thomas W.: *1-2-3 Magic*, Child Management Inc., Glen Ellyn, Illinois, 1995

Pogrebin, Letty Cottin: *Growing Up Free,* Bantam Books, New York, 1980

Satir, Virginia: *Peoplemaking,* Science and Behavioral Books Inc., Palo Alto, California, 1972.

Schmidt, Fran and Friedman, Alice: *Fighting Fair in Families,* Peace Education Foundation, Miami, Florida, 1990

Spock, Benjamin: *Baby and Child Care* (6th Edition), Dutton Pocket Books, New York, 1992

Stewart, Jack C.: *Counseling Parents of Exceptional Children,* Charles E. Merrill Publishing Company, Columbus, Ohio, 1978

Watterson, Bill: Assorted *Calvin and Hobbes* Collections, Andrews McMeel Publishing, Kansas City.

About the Author

Dr. **Maggie Mamen** is a psychologist in private practice in Nepean, Ontario, who specializes in working with children, adolescents and their families. She gives frequent workshops and seminars and has taught university courses on child development and exceptional children since 1981.

Maggie wrote her first book *Who's in Charge? A Guide to Family Management* in 1997 at the request of parents and teachers who attended her presentations. That book sparked numerous guest spots on radio, television and in print in all parts of the country, including CTV's national show *Canada AM*.

Originally from London, England, Maggie came to Canada with her husband Rolf in 1971. The couple have three adult children.

———•———

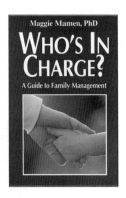

Who's in Charge?
A Guide to Family Management
Dr. Maggie Mamen
0-921165-47-1
$16.95 CAN $14.95 U.S.

Many families run into problems when they find themselves with a Child in Charge, whether that child is a toddler or a teen. In *Who's in Charge?*, Dr. Mamen uses the metaphor of running a small company—with parents as senior "management" and children as valued "trainees"—to provide an easy-to-read, troubleshooting approach for parents who wish to regain control and give themselves permission to parent with both warmth and clear guidelines.

Who's in Charge? is available in bookstores or directly from
Creative Bound Inc. at 1-800-287-8610 (toll-free in North America)
www.creativebound.com